Managing
the
madness

A Practical Guide to Middle Grades Classrooms

Jack C. Berckemeyer

National Middle School Association

Betty Edwards, Executive Director
April Tibbles, Director of Publications
Carla Weiland, Publications Editor
John Lounsbury, Editor, Professional Publications
Dawn Williams, Publications Manager
Lindsay Kronmiller, Graphic Designer
Jonathan Starr, Graphic Designer
Marcia Meade-Hurst, Senior Publications Representative
Peggy Rajala, Publications & Event Marketing Manager

National Middle School Association
4151 Executive Parkway, Suite 300
Westerville, Ohio 43081
1-800-528-NMSA f: 614-895-4750
www.nmsa.org

Foreword

There are moments with Jack Berckemeyer when I think I'm in the presence of absolute genius; he's a dynamo that never fails to inspire. Using everyday classroom realities, Jack cultivates our instructional potential, using acts of kindness, stunning wit, and vibrant applications of the middle school concept. And just as refreshing, there are other times when Jack is an overgrown adolescent who is making good on his promise to his teachers that he'd one day rule the educational universe and inject it with a healthy dose of warped and wonderful humor. We are lucky to be in his orbit.

Jack gives the latest research in teaching young adolescents life through his large repertoire of personal anecdotes, uncanny comprehension of student and teacher psychology, and real-teaching savvy. He is up there with John Lounsbury, Nancy Doda, and Paul George as a consummate ambassador for middle level education. I've never seen someone wed the big ideas of education with their requisite details so skillfully and compel us to do the same.

We've all been begging Jack to unleash his turbo-powered, teaching acumen upon the world in a book format for years, and now he's finally done it. In these pages you'll find innovative and specific ideas on discipline, humor, technology integration, seating arrangements, student-teacher interaction, bulletin boards, attention grabbers, classroom management, and much more. He tackles the most awkward situations that arise in middle level classrooms that are not often considered in other books. His responses are full of, "Why didn't we think of that?" common sense, but they also push us to color outside the lines, and our teacher's craft is all the more beautiful for it. This will be among the first books I give to new teachers and to seasoned education colleagues I respect.

Some of the legendary stories that Jack shares in his training sessions are included, and his unique voice comes through every word. I lost count of the number of times I nodded in agreement and laughed aloud while reading these ideas. How does this man get inside the minds of young adolescents so well and tell their truth so powerfully? And how does he do the same with the adults who guide them? Jack operates daily on a wavelength many of us can only dream of experiencing.

Through this book we can now bring Jack to each team meeting, give him to colleagues in need of hope and creativity, and use his wisdom to feed our teaching souls. He demonstrates the people and pedagogy connections that help us reach increasingly diverse adolescents and stay in the profession. We now have no choice but to teach like this is the only day we get with our students; every moment counts. Let's enjoy where Jack places us — in the driver's seat of the school bus — while he rides in the back, grinning and bouncing high as he teaches us with every bump of the road. 'No signed permission slip needed: This is a trip every middle school teacher should take.

—Rick Wormeli, September 2009

Rick is a teacher trainer, columnist for NMSA's *Middle Ground*, and author of *Meet Me in the Middle, Day One and Beyond, Summarization in any Subject, Fair Isn't Always Equal, Differentiation: From Planning to Practice,* and *Metaphors & Analogies: Power Tools for Teaching any Subject.*

Contents

And the "thank you" goes to.......

Creating this book was truly a journey for me. Because there are so few times you can thank people in print who have positively influenced your life, and this might be my one and only book, I thank those who pushed me, encouraged me, and made me sound so wonderful.

Thanks to the editing team at National Middle School Association: April Tibbles, Carla Weiland, and Cheri Howman. You did a great job. On a personal note, thanks to Joel Showalter, you are a dear friend for helping me sound like me.

To my mentors Pete Lorain and Sue Swaim: It is all your fault!

I am also appreciative of the entire staff at National Middle School Association: You are amazing. To Pam Kuntz and Holly Holland: Thanks for making me do this!

To my past teammates at Scott Carpenter: Thanks for making me laugh every day. A big thanks to Jan Blatchford, Zerphayne Willis, Annette Fante and Susie DeSmit for your support and friendship.

Thanks to Patricia Yellico, Tina Cerventes, and Roberta Fromhart for being the best middle school teachers a future middle school speaker could ever have.

Finally, this book is dedicated to my parents, Jack and Sharon Berckemeyer, for paying for my college education and for their constant love and support: I am proud to be your son!!!

A special dedication to Phyllis Shotts: We miss you, friend. You played a major role in my life and the lives of our friends! Gone way too soon!

To the consultants, teachers, and administrators who make a huge impact on the lives of young adolescents, I say, "Thanks!"

Preface
It's True, Honest!

Every educator has a story about how he or she got that first teaching job. Some simply applied, interviewed, and got the job. Others spent hours researching the job market. Some just looked in their own hometowns, while others sought adventure and explored moving halfway around the world.

Hired in the middle of the school year and right out of college, I had just finished my student teaching. Out of the blue I got a call from Scott Carpenter Middle School in Adams County School District, Denver, Colorado. Like so many struggling new teachers, I lived in my parents' basement, which was about 60 miles away in Colorado Springs. I had been planning on substitute teaching and then looking for a job close to home. Growing up, I rode the school bus 10 miles to school in a rural part of Colorado. There were 85 people in my graduating class. In my wildest dreams I never thought I would get a job in the big, bad city of Denver.

As was typical in those days, I was interviewed by eight people, three of whom were my future teammates. In addition, the principal, assistant principal, and the guidance counselor joined us. There they sat, my future teammates—my potential support system! Ms. Tossava, who taught social studies; Ms. Trumbo, the best special education teacher ever; and a gentleman by the name of Mr. Gassman, who taught science. What kind of middle school teacher has the name Gassman?! I always made sure I pronounced his name with an extra special emphasis on each part of his name—Gas Man. They were all a joy to work with; their humor and caring made my first year a success.

It became apparent during the interview that humor would play a huge part in our team's dynamics if I got the job. The interview was going along well until, while I was answering a question enthusiastically, a big drop of spit flew out of my mouth and landed well toward the middle of the table. When I get excited, I spit. I guess I get too keyed up and forget to swallow. So, as the spit gleamed on the table, everyone started looking at the spit and not at me. I felt like I had lost all control of the interview—so I did what any good teacher would do, I diverted their attention by putting my hand over the spit. Then, further excited, I inadvertently pulled my hand back, smearing the spit. The point, however, is, I got the job—much to the questioning looks and laughter from my principal, future teammates, and the counselor, who, I had figured out by then, was present to assist me should I suffer a nervous breakdown.

Because I was the newbie, I had to teach an "elective exploratory" class, which the principal told me would be an eighth grade language arts class. I know you are thinking the same thing I asked my principal: "Since when is eighth grade language arts an exploratory class?" The answer is one that all middle level educators need to watch out for. My principal replied, "They are a unique group of kids." He rather casually mentioned that about half the students were gifted and talented, and the other half had criminal records. During that first semester teaching the one eighth grade language arts/exploratory class, I realized that I could not tell which students were the criminals and which were gifted. Because I was hired in the middle of the year, teachers from the other teams chose which of their students to give to me. You can imagine the types of students I was blessed to receive; I knew I had to start off with a bang and lay down the law right away.

Yes, that first year was a struggle for me and for my students. It is not easy being a new teacher; most of the time, it is learning by trial and error, and boy did I make a lot of errors. Placed in a classroom in the middle of the year with little time to prepare, I had to face students who had been voted off the island, and I had a class made up of intelligent criminals.

What helped me succeed that year was a combination of factors—great students, good mentors, outstanding colleagues and mentors, a supportive team, patient-with-me parents, and a music, P.E., and art teacher, who all supported me. Thank you, Ms. Blatchford, Ms. Willis, and Mrs. DeSmit. My sense of humor and my dedication to teaching young adolescents helped me the most. But in reality, perhaps what saved me from quitting was a strong sense of classroom management, based on consistency, respect, and the ability to listen and laugh every day. For those mentored me and offered advice regarding classroom management, I am forever thankful.

Introduction

Although colleges and universities try conscientiously to prepare fledgling middle school teachers for handling classroom management, try as they do, it seems this is one area of teaching that just has to be learned on the job.

Classroom management is about trial and error; it comes through practice, patience, teamwork, flexibility, quality mentoring, willingness to seek help when needed, and a huge dose of humor. Each teacher's particular personality influences his or her teaching style. Sometimes, the best inspirations come from planning and thoughtfulness. However, most come from sheer, dumb luck.

This book does not offer the one solution for all situations—it is a free-flowing discussion of ideas based on my experiences to help the middle grades classroom teacher get through daily rounds of uprisings, hostage situations (with demands), commotions, and chaos. (Please note that some of my examples are really humorous asides and should not to be taken literally.) Most of the strategies can be easily adapted and effectively implemented by any middle grades educator.

Readers will readily realize that the book's strategies reflect my personality; you must discern which ideas fit comfortably with your personality and teaching style. Never try to be someone you are not in the classroom. Practice patience. Seek out excellent seasoned teachers—a wealth of knowledge.

If a team study group or an entire faculty is reading this book at the same time, look for solutions that the whole team or all teams can implement and accomplish as a unit. Each section of the book offers background and advice based on my experiences or observations as a middle level educator. Feel free to make modifications to fit your personal teaching style and classroom. A tremendous resource is *Inventing Powerful Pedagogy: Share. 'Steal'. Revise. Own.* (2009). Author Ross Burkhardt describes how good teachers learn to spot good ideas and transform them into their own powerful teaching resources.

There is no one solution or strategy for every classroom management problem that will occur. Try new ideas, take time to listen to your students, trust your instincts, and most important—have some fun along the way. School is a serious place for learning, but it can also be a place filled with humor and laughter—which, incidentally, will lead to higher achievement—research says so.

chapter 1

Rule #1: Engage Them

Mr. Berckemeyer, I need to walk around the room at least ten times an hour. It helps me focus.

Middle schools would be radically different if every adolescent entered puberty at the same date and time. Imagine teaching young adolescents and saying, "OK, in five, four, three, two, one—everyone has now left childhood; welcome to young adolescence!" However, it just does not work that way; adolescents are on their own timelines. See *Promoting Harmony: Young Adolescent Development and Classroom Practices,* Third Edition by Strahan, L'Esperance, and Van Hoose (2009) for a detailed description of the physical, emotional, social, and intellectual development of young adolescents. Suffice it to say: middle school teachers' lives do not lack for moments of high drama brought about by their students' development.

As adolescents go through changes, they experience increases in twitching, a constant need for movement, and rapid mood swings. They can go from having vast amounts of energy at their desks to sleeping on the floor. You can assign a silent reading activity and then watch a young adolescent male make the most unique facial expressions while his arm is swinging around in the air. Seemingly unable to control his body movements, he lets out a gigantic, loud sigh that could cause a tsunami halfway across the world. If you summon the courage to ask him whether he is all right, he looks at you and says, "WHAT." He is totally clueless that he has released an enormous amount of energy in a short period of time. Teachers must help adolescents understand the vast changes they are experiencing are entirely normal.

Maintaining an awareness of the significance of their changes may help young adolescents weather the tumultuous middle school years. Here are some great ways to keep both you and your students aware of their rapid growth spurts during a school year.

- At the year's beginning, take individual photos of your students next to a poster that will hang for the entire year. Take photos of the students next to that poster again at the end of the year. You and the students will be able to see how much they have grown and changed in just nine months.

- Have students put a piece of string under their shoes and extend the string to the top of their heads. Cut the string, roll it up, and attach a piece tape to it with the students' names. Return the strings at the end of the year. I guarantee you will have at least one student say, "Ms. Rios, this is not my string." Meanwhile you are thinking, "Is your name on the string? Then it is yours. What does he think? I came in and changed the names?" Students will be surprised at how the string now only goes to their shoulders or their noses. In the case of those students whose strings are the same size they were the beginning of the year, tell them to check for growth during the next year—adolescents are on different timelines. I did think it was strange once when a student's string was bigger than he was. Maybe he actually did shrink that year.

Need for movement

Many educators have moved away from focusing on adolescent development due, in part, to the intense focus on high-stakes testing and the increased emphasis on content. Great middle level educators know that you need both—content knowledge and development knowledge. For example, do you know that at the onset of puberty the lower part of adolescents' spines fuse together and that this can make it uncomfortable to sit for long periods? Could this be why they get up to move around the room at various times? Could this explain why the pencil is never sharpened enough? Or why the piece of paper needs to be placed in the trash can during the most important part of your lesson? Could this be why they rock in their chairs while you feel the need to chant, "Four on the floor?" (Meanwhile several students are thinking, "It is really six legs, if you count my legs.")

It is a simple fact: Adolescents will move, with or without permission. Our goal is to get them to move with purpose. When I taught sixth grade, I had students who would just walk around for no reason. When I asked, "Do you need something?" Or "Can I help you?" they would just look at me and say, "No I am fine, I am just walking around." Totally oblivious, they were invariably standing right in front of me while I was trying to teach. That is when I began the habit of pulling large clumps of hair from my head! I had failed to realize I needed to give them opportunities and a purpose for moving around.

Suggestions for incorporating movement and keeping students engaged include:

- Dry erase boards can be a teacher's best friend. Place one under every student's desk. When you ask a question, students can write their answers on the dry erase boards; if they do not know the answer, they can draw a question mark. When they are done, ask them to use both hands to hold the boards up in the air as high as they can reach. This forces them to stretch and sit up straight. In addition to engaging academically, they are physically active in a positive way.

- Having students stand up next to their desks if they support a statement or an answer gets them moving and keeps them focused on the lesson.

- Have students clap twice if the answer is A and clap three times if it is B. Again, a simple movement can help encourage participation.

- Come up with a catchphrase or statement relevant to your lesson. Tell students that when you use it, they can respond with some appropriate gesture, noise, or chant. For example, whenever I said the phrase "mad scientist" in a lesson on science fiction, the students could shout BOO-HA-HA. Yes, it seems strange. But it was great for finding out if students were paying attention. Saying it randomly, I always hoped my students were paying attention, but often the only response I got was the hissing noise from the outdated heating unit in the corner of my room. Then suddenly a student would snap out of her education coma and do the BOO-HA-HA, causing others to return to this planet and follow suit. Eventually, the class would perk up and start paying attention.

- At a specified time have the students jump up out of their seats and move two seats to the right.

- Have students shelve their journals or help pass out books.

- Do row relays for reviewing items on the board.

- The next time you are teaching and you realize that your students have been sitting more than 20 minutes, come up with something that forces them to move. They need the change of pace, and it just might decrease the number of random walkabouts during the most important part of a lesson. Allowing students to move keeps them engaged and alert and is key to a middle level teacher's success (and sanity).

"I'm bored."

A typical dream for a middle level teacher is to see every student in the class sitting on the edge of his or her seat anticipating knowledge on a daily basis. The reality is no matter how hard you prepare for the lesson, no matter how many things you blow up or dissect, there will always be that one student who says, "We did this last year, and this is boring. I hate this class." Young adolescents are born to be bored, and often it is not perceived as cool to love school. Yes, this means that middle school students will not get excited about the cool multi-color tiles for math. But it does not mean you should stick with handouts; just don't be surprised when they do not react the way you anticipated.

When young adolescents get bored, they look for ways to entertain themselves. Usually this means involving someone nearby, so they tend to poke, pull, or trip anyone who gets near them. A popular ways to alleviate boredom is the pencil-is-not-sharpened-enough routine which can be performed while you are teaching, during silent reading, or at any other time during the class period. The student gets up and walks toward the pencil sharpener, making a few stops along the way to disrupt others by knocking their papers on the floor, messing with their hair, or even giving them a slight shove. Having arrived at the pencil sharpener, the student makes as many attempts as needed to get the pencil sharp enough to use as a dart. Then begins the long journey back to his seat—this time using a different route and causing disruptions and distractions in a different part of the room.

One way to reduce adolescent boredom is to ensure that your classroom strategies are targeted to meet the needs of students with a variety of learning styles. To determine if there are needs you are not presently addressing, try the following activity in which you will match your lessons to the characteristics of young adolescents outlined in *This We Believe: Keys to Educating Young Adolescents* (2010). Some of the areas might be challenging, and you may want to consult with your teammates for ideas. Ideas you generate for this activity can be classroom activities, expectations, policies, procedures, lessons, or ways you interact with your students.

Figure 1-1. The Developmentally Responsive Classroom

List the activities, lessons, and methods you use that relate to the characteristics of middle grades students.

Characteristic	Example
Rapid growth changes	
Restlessness, need for physical activity	
Intensely curious	

Figure 1-1 (continued)

Characteristic	Example
Prefer active to passive learning	
Real-life learning situations/ connections	
Issues related to peer pressure	
Issues related to morals	
Dealing with shades of gray	
Compassion for self and others	
Vocal about inconsistencies	
Self-absorbed	
Seek independence	
Self-esteem issues/ self-conscious	
Seek recognition	
Often over-react	
Like fads and pop culture	

Figure 1-1 (continued)

Characteristic	Example
Need time alone	
Need to build positive relationships with peers	
Mood swings	
Bullying and other harassment issues	
Developing new beliefs and attitudes	
Seek new academic challenges	
Need organizational ideas and strategies	
Seek one-on-one time with teacher	
Creative expression	
Structure and clear limits	
Opportunities for self-definition	

After doing the activity and increasing your awareness of your strengths and weaknesses in matching your teaching to the characteristics of young adolescents, check out the imaginative, interactive learning activities suggested in Jill Spencer's book *Everyone's Invited! Interactive Strategies That Engage Young Adolescents* (2008).

Herding cats

The worst teaching days seem to come out of nowhere. Just when you think things are going well, something happens. It happens so quickly you are left standing there with nine pencils sticking out of your hair thinking, "I just said, 'Move to a quiet place in the room for this next activity.' It seemed simple enough; it seemed like nothing could go wrong; and yet, the next thing I knew, three kids were pushing each other, and two girls were crying. How could that happen in less than three minutes?"

Sometimes the simplest tasks are the most painful. Every middle grades teacher knows that getting young adolescents to start a task can be like trying to herd a dozen cats in the same direction. Educators need to know there is no one surefire way to keep young adolescents focused and on task. However, there are multiple methods to help keep things moving along in an orderly manner.

Grouping students

Putting students into groups can be a two-minute ordeal or may cause friction for an entire grading period. Your day as a middle grades teacher is not complete unless you hear "Is this the same group as last week" or "What group am I in again?" or,

> " Adapting your teaching methods to match the range of young adolescents' characteristics can, at times, be frustrating because their abilities and strengths are as varied as their shoe sizes. "

my personal favorite, "I hate my group!" Even if you plan well, you will have confusion and commotion. Being consistent helps, as does telling students your expectations before having them move about the room.

Assigning students to groups

Grouping can be based on data about students' performances in previous grades, special programs they participated in, their level of study and research skills, behavioral strengths and weaknesses, and academic strengths and weaknesses. Alternately, you can form groups by putting a playing card on every student's desk and having students find other group members with the same card in all the suits. Or form groups by lining the students up by height and then having them number off. There are tons of ways to group kids, so change it up and keep it interesting!

Moving to their groups

Display group members' names on the overhead. Even better, write them on large pieces of paper and post them around the room, giving students a reason to walk around and find their groups. Yes, it will be loud, even a little crazy, so have them stand up, and have them make sure they have all their materials before they move to another part of the room. This will avoid their making constant trips to their original seats. Then give them a purpose for moving by giving them specific directions, making a visual check to see if they are ready, and then giving them the cue to move to their groups. Set a time limit and make it fun: tell students they have 40 seconds to get to their new location and group. Do an exaggerated countdown—be "over the top" so that they will move more quickly to their seats. It might resemble the running of the bulls in Pamplona, Spain, but it is effective.

Some teachers use music for transition time; students learn the music that is played during specific activities, and their response to the music becomes automatic. The styles of music for the different activities should be distinct enough that students are certain to what they are transitioning.

Working in Groups

Even if students have worked in groups in previous years, tell them your expectations for the different roles played by group members (recorder, leader, etc.) Later on in the year, after you see how the group members are working together, you can let the students have more input in deciding group makeup.

Even while working in groups, unless they are getting supplies or checking directions that are posted, they should be seated and attentive. If you have assigned the groups, put their graded papers at their new location or put sticky notes on their desks so that they know exactly where to go; make it possible and probable for them to be in their seats ready to work when the bell rings. Have them place book bags and purses against one wall after they get papers and pencils out. Students are NOT to be eating, texting, or playing with "stuff" of any kind.

What to do while students are in a group

Your roaming will prevent their roaming; never sit at the teacher's desk when students are in groups! Continuously move around the room, never staying in the same place very long. Also, keep your head up. While this may sound like a strange piece of advice, you would be surprised how many times teachers look down and miss interesting social behaviors occurring around the room. Keeping your head up increases your perception and visual skills and allows you to monitor behavior in the classroom. Who knows, you might actually develop eyes in the back of your head if you keep your head up. Plus, it helps keep young adolescents on task.

When we take for granted that young adolescents hear our expectations, we miss the opportunity to address multiple learning styles; let them *see* the expectations as well. Go over the directions for the group work by starting with a student from one group giving the first step, a student from another group giving the next step, etc., until they are all covered. Ensure that each person in each group has been assigned a job and knows how to do it.

List your expectations for the groups in several areas—on the board, on the overhead, and in a handout for each group of students. Then, during the activity, when you are asked for instructions, you can point out where the students are in the process and help students learn to track their way through the activity. Go over the directions for the group work by starting with a student from one group giving the first step, a student from another group giving the next step, and continue until all steps are covered. Ensure that each person in each group has been assigned a job and knows how to do it.

After placing students in their new groups, you need tools to deal with the issues that arise while they are working together. Group work roadblocks change daily and can include students off task, a group member not working, students wandering around the room bothering other groups, and—the most common—one group that is not even close to being done when all other groups have finished. Handle each situation individually. Constantly check the progress of the groups, moving troubled groups closer to you, and do not hesitate to remove students who are major distractions to their groups.

Also, you need to realize that when young adolescents are in a group, they *will* socialize. It is part of who they are; they crave interaction with their peers. Their need to laugh, debate, and argue in groups helps build social skills and social norms— a critical part of their development. Students with special concerns can be placed facing the teacher or with their backs to the teacher so that they don't know when the teacher is there. Friends can be placed back to back.

In Rick Wormeli's book *Differentiation: From Planning to Practice* (2007), Rick describes in detail how to use flexible grouping to meet the needs of a wide range of learners within the same classroom. His time-tested strategies and reflective advice about differentiated instruction are an invaluable resource in managing the middle school classroom.

Although these are simple ideas and seem quite obvious, in many classrooms I have observed teachers looking down and never leaving one spot. I admit to starting my own teaching career head down and lost. It took about three weeks for me to learn that, to see everything, I had to ignore the ugly carpeting and look around the room. Even worse, thinking the overhead projector needed me, I rarely left its side. Maintaining eye contact with my students and moving around the classroom made me a better teacher, because I did not miss a thing transpiring in the room. As you know, issues can crop up at the speed of light, and you need to make sure you are a witness to the event and know the back story. In addition to freeing you up for managing the class, having the students handle the overhead, interactive whiteboard, and computer keeps them focused.

Releasing students

Never let students leave the room until you have dismissed them. Using a consistent phrase as a signal for the students to change classes makes a huge difference. You can check the floor and room before you say your magical words. As you walk around the room, you can tell students to pick up trash (or get up off the floor.) Once the room is clean, you can say whatever phrase you have chosen. Students can then pack up and leave for their next class. You and the next class get a clean room, and students leave in an orderly manner. Sample release phrases include:

- Have a nice day!
- Ciao, Bambinos!
- Hasta la vista, baby.
- Later, alligators.
- Thanks for your hard work today.
- Get out! (Not a good choice, but sometimes we are thinking it.)
- See you later.
- Have a good one!
- The room looks good, so you may leave.

You could also dismiss the class by groups such as students wearing blue, those with black tennis shoes, those with hazel eyes, or those with first names that begin with a certain letter. Mix it up and be creative. Use your phrase with the groups as well, every day. No exceptions! It sets the tone and helps you with consistency. You can also offer friendly reminders while they wait to be released: "Don't forget to check your assignment book and the assignment board, and bring in your moldy science project."

Questions for Reflection

1. For what characteristics of young adolescents from Figure 1-1 did you lack examples or have few examples? With a colleague, brainstorm appropriate activities that would appeal to the characteristics you need to address.

2. Try a new strategy for grouping students or otherwise getting students moving with purpose. Observe carefully how students react, and when you try it again, remove any sources of confusion in your directions.

3. Have a trusted colleague observe your body language while you teach; do you tend to put your head down? Do you tend to stay in one place?

4. How often do you move around the room to monitor class behavior?

5. What are three different ways to organize students into groups?

chapter II

Show You Care: Attention, Humor, Trends

Mr. Berckemeyer, this time I promise to ask a meaningful question.

Young adolescents look for attention from their peers, parents, and teachers. Although not a single question may be asked while you are teaching a lesson, at the bell you may find yourself surrounded by nine smiling students standing ready to critique your choice of clothing: "I don't like your sweater" or "Those shoes are cool." How many times do you have to chase them out of the room so you can get ready for the next class? They crave adult interaction, which is critical to adolescent development. Being around you affirms their beliefs, allows them to use humor, and most important, it makes them feel older and more mature. Your willingness to listen to young adolescents is key to your success as a teacher. Let middle school students know they are valued, and don't be afraid to smile as you share the precious commodity of time with them.

Adolescents want attention—positive or negative. Have you ever had your praise of a young adolescent backfire? "Gee, Reyna I am so glad you finished that assignment." Looking right at you she says, "It was so easy and stupid—anyone could have done it." Or "Mr. Berckemeyer, you are such a dork. And you need a Tic-Tac." During this exchange you are thinking, "Wait a minute; I am trying to be nice. I am giving praise, I am acknowledging that she is doing a good job, and in return she is being rude and disrespectful."

Understand that attention is attention, and sometimes students who are familiar with only negative attention will naturally know how to seek only negative attention. It is the same for the students who are constantly seeking your praise and attention. When a perfect student completes an assignment within five minutes of your giving it and they get in your face asking, "What can I do? What can I do?" You think, "You can get out of my face and sit down." But because you realize the student needs your affirmation and attention, you refrain from the emotional response.

Thoughts on dealing with attention:
- First of all, there are times you need to jump up on a chair and shout out loud about how awesome a student's work sample is. But the rule of thumb is that

you must know your students. For some, that would be devastating and overwhelming.

- Make sure you get the students' permission before you use their work. Sometimes they might not feel comfortable with you sharing their thoughts and feelings.

- For students who struggle with praise, you might just give them eye contact and say in a low voice, "Nice work." Next time you might give them a low-key high five or pat on the back. Even better, wait till the class is over, call them over, and say how proud of them you are. Make it subtle. Never go overboard.

- For other students, it might be a warm, comforting smile or a slight head nod. Use their name in an example. Have them share an answer with the class.

- The best way to give praise is to find something positive to say to every student as you walk around the room sometime during each week.

- Everyone wants praise and seeks approval from the teacher. And every student deserves a teacher who will provide them with encouragement and praise.

They want attention, and if they do not get it at home or elsewhere, they will seek it from you, their teacher. Lessons that use their reflecting skills give them room to explore and communicate their needs for attention and interaction; journals are another way for students to raise issues and topics important to them that the class can talk about.

The next time a student asks you a question such as "What are we doing today?" "Are we doing anything fun?" Or "Where is the homework basket?" remember that in many cases they obviously do know the answer to the question. What they seek rather than an answer is your attention; they truly are not trying to drive you insane. However, some days it is a short drive!

One form of attention: Humor

Often, as classroom teachers we are in one of our finest moments—teaching the solar system or how the earth is changing—and just when we have every student in the palm of our hands, some wise young adolescent will make a funny comment that is truly not appropriate. Usually, the comment involves one of the following words—gas, balls, or a reference to a planet that sounds like the word anus. Everyone laughs, while you with the straight face will say, "Nicolas, that is not funny." Meanwhile you are thinking, "I need to write this down! They will SO love this in the faculty lounge!"

Young adolescents struggle with humor—they are not sure when it is appropriate to share their unique and sometimes warped sense of humor. And you might struggle with knowing when it is okay for you to let down your guard and crack a smile. We fear letting things get too out-of-hand and losing control. However, some of the best advice you will ever receive about teaching young adolescents is to go ahead and enjoy their humor; it is okay to laugh. Just look at the way they interact with each other, not to mention what they say, or their ever-changing hairstyles and colors.

"Remember, anything is worth a try—you can only dress up and sing so many times in a year before your colleagues start to think that you have lost it and should retire early."

Those of us who have been teaching and dealing with young adolescents for a long time realize the untruths we have been told. For example, "There is no such thing as a stupid question." How many of us get at least five stupid questions a day? Sometimes these off-the-wall questions come from students, sometimes from parents, and even from our teammates. Humor helps us respond appropriately to unique, bizarre statements and questions and daily frustrations. Although teachers should not ever point and laugh at a student or ridicule a student, enjoying a good laugh can be therapeutic for both you and students. Be considerate in using students' nicknames, and only use them with the students' permission and if you feel it is appropriate.

My motto is: if you do not laugh at least five times a day in a middle school, there is something wrong with you. Enjoy the ups and downs of working with young adolescents—ride the roller coaster ride. Here are some things I've learned about young adolescents' senses of humor.

- Their humor is ever-changing and evolving.
- They can be overly sensitive regarding humor. Build relationships with your students so you know to what they can adjust.

- Never take their humor personally. They can and do use humor to attack each other and even the teacher. When humor is rude or demeaning, address it right away.

- Don't be afraid to laugh at yourself. If you do something funny, laugh about it.

- There is nothing funnier than watching your teacher do something silly. Slapstick comedy works for young adolescents. This does not mean that you should light your tie or shirt sleeve on fire with the Bunsen burner—that is just scary and dangerous.

Humor is part of your personality, and if you use it wisely and mindfully, that humor can reduce stress for you and your students and build necessary bonds with them. Expressing humor shows young adolescents that you care about them and you enjoy being around them.

Stages of humor and the issue of sarcasm

In developing their senses of humor, students typically start with simple jokes, such as knock-knock jokes or one-liners they have read in a joke book. They won't understand some of the jokes; some they will realize have negative or stereotypical punch lines; and some have sexual connotations. Then, as they progress to the next stage of humor, they will look for ways to embarrass and humiliate their peers, the teacher, or anyone close by. They find embarrassment funny, so they clap when someone drops a tray of food in the lunch room, and they giggle when someone trips and falls. These are normal stages for most young adolescents. Understand that some might skip these stages or (even worse) get stuck in a certain stage for most of their adult lives.

The final stage for young adolescents is the sarcasm stage. Young adolescents use sarcasm, a tough issue to address, on a daily basis: they use it toward each other, toward the teacher, or toward one of their assignments. Theories abound that eighth grade girls developed sarcasm. In fact, many of them use sarcasm wordlessly. All it takes is one look, a flick of the hair, or a wrinkled-up nose, and you know you have done something wrong. Ever been standing in the hallway doing hall duty and have an eighth grade girl walk by and cut you down to size with a look, hair flick, or dagger stare that could cut glass? They might not even be aware of doing this. It's just a normal adolescent moment. Hopefully, they will outgrow it—at least a majority of them.

Other forms of humor connect to real-life situations, have a deeper meaning, or have multiple meanings. Can some adolescents get to those stages? Yes, not many, but a few. Most young adolescents have difficulty understanding some deeper levels of humor so they may not laugh at something that seems extremely funny to you.

Teachers' use of sarcasm

While humor can help deflect tension and decrease classroom issues, it can also escalate a situation with students. Plus, many teachers are not comfortable with it. The truth is: everyone has a sense of humor. Everyone has the ability to laugh. You first start with the ability to laugh at yourself. Inevitably, without trying, you will do some of the most embarrassing things in front of young adolescents as their teacher. It is up to you to decide on how to handle it. You can yell at your class and tell them it is not funny, or you can realize you made a mistake, have a good laugh together, and move on. Although you cannot teach someone to be funny, you can encourage and use laughter.

Leading experts say to never use sarcasm with your students. True, a teacher must never humiliate a student; do not embarrass them or make them feel inferior. However, basic forms of sarcasm can work if you have a great relationship with your class and the student that is the object of the sarcasm. *This is a very fine line for many educators.* Some do a great job because they can use the strategy largely toward themselves and in little doses with their students. For you to be sarcastic with yourself requires high self-esteem and the ability to laugh at yourself. Never use sarcasm as your main form of humor. Yes, you can use one-liner jokes and deeper levels of humor, but be sensitive to your individual students and the class as a whole. Most middle school students recognize sarcasm for what it really is: a weapon. Teachers must take care when using it.

Another form of attention: Keeping up with fads, trends, and slang

Staying in tune with the fads, fashions, and trends of young adolescents shows you care enough about your students to really find out who they are. This is challenging due to the likelihood of fads changing in 24 hours. Guidelines for awareness of adolescents' trends:

- Yes, to know their fads, fashions, trends, and slang means you might have to watch current popular television shows and movies. Sometimes it can be painful. However, adolescents are always flabbergasted when you make a reference to current pop culture and you connect to them.

- Use appropriate pop cultural references of which there are multitudes, and relate them to classroom life. For example, next time you get so angry the veins in your neck begin to throb, just use a *Survivor* reference and tell the student, "You are off the island." Although it might seem strange, the mood in the classroom might lighten.

- Getting a class back on track might mean breaking out into a current pop song. If you can't sing, that's even better.

- Pay attention to the newest movies and television shows. Make references that support what you might be teaching with a movie line or television catchphrase.

- How many times have you been teaching when a student says something, and you are not sure whether or not it is appropriate? Although you may act cool, students can tell you are clueless. When you hear an unfamiliar phrase or word, see if others know the meaning. If all else fails, find a young adolescent willing to spill the beans.

- Be aware of changing trends in clothing—and this can happen very quickly. How many of you remember slap bracelets and girls with bangs so high they needed a building permit? The only fad that has stayed around for a long period of time is sagging pants, which, at last check, has been popular for 20 years now. That is the longest educational trend ever. I am not sure even phonics lasted that long!

Adolescents want to be unique at the same time they are similar to other adolescents around the world. They listen to the same music, watch the same shows, and play the same video games. And more important, they tell the same jokes and laugh at the same things.

Once I asked a group of 10 eighth graders if they knew who Elvis Presley was. You may expect that only a few knew of Elvis, however, all 10 knew who he was. Then I asked a group of over 100 teachers how many had heard of Black Eyed Peas. Surprisingly, only about 10 teachers had heard of that rock group. Granted, the 10 knowing the group were under the age of 25. It is interesting that young adolescents know our culture, but we have little concept of theirs.

Have you in your teacher role ever been called a something that led you to wonder whether or not it was appropriate? A big concern for most middle level educators, inappropriate phrases and slang have become commonplace in our schools; in fact in many cases using them is the norm and acceptable. One example of a phrase formerly unacceptable that is now a common aspect of school life is young adolescents' use of the word "sucks." Students often describe lessons by saying they suck or are stupid. Another common pejorative is "gay." When they hear these words, many teachers have no response; is it because we as educators just don't hear it? Or are we consumed with so many other things that we just let it pass? Do we think, "You have to pick your battles, and this isn't one I'm picking"? .

Teachers, administrators, and even parents must teach students that these words used in a mean manner can be offensive and should not be allowed in our hallways and classrooms. Should we be frightened by the changes we are seeing, or should we embrace them? This is a difficult question because there are many possible answers. We could spend days talking about how we as educators must pick up the slack of society and teach everything from math to manners. As we teachers help facilitate change in our society, we are in some cases a moral compass for our students. Studies have shown that many young adolescents get their beliefs and values not only from family and friends but from their teachers as well. Thinking of us as role models can be frightening—I have seen what teachers can do in front of a karaoke machine!

How to address inappropriate slang:
- Never pretend you did not hear a rude comment or off-color remark—address it immediately. No exceptions!
- Explain to students why certain words and not appropriate in the school setting. This is no different

than our not allowing hats in the building or any other policy or school-wide rule.

- The first week of school terms and terminology must be the focus of a lesson; have a thorough discussion of your expectations for acceptable language for formal and informal writing and for talking; make sure students know that the discussion marks the beginning of everyone using appropriate language the rest of the year.

- If you hear a new word and are unsure of its meaning, you can quickly find out by asking students or watching MTV. Prepare yourself for shock.

- Discuss new slang at faculty meetings—many staff members will be grateful to know that they can stop saying, "Thank you," when a student calls them that word they do not understand.

- Address slang in a proactive way. No longer can we think: "I don't know if that word is appropriate or not." If we do not address some of these issues now, what words will be next?

Questions for Reflection

1. Keep a record of how many students you can give personal feedback or attention to in a day; it need not be public praise—any form of personal attention counts. See whether you can reach as many of your students in a week as possible in one way or another.

2. Observe your students' developing senses of humor; how does this impact the style of humor you use with them? Can you recall ever resorting to sarcasm that, though not intentionally hurtful, was not the best decision?

3. From what television program, magazine, radio station, movie, etc. that is widely viewed by young adolescents can you learn about them?

4. List your methods for keeping current regarding adolescent trends and fads.

5. Are you finding middle grades a fun place to be? Do you laugh every day?

chapter III

Design the Environment

Mr. Berckemeyer, I can't see the board with Shannon's big head in the way!

C ould it be time to really take a look at your classroom, at the physical arrangement and "decor?" Do you need to redesign and discard outdated materials? Could your students offer ideas on how to make some basic changes to the walls and even the ceiling? Your classroom is a reflection of you and your students—maybe it is time to give it a makeover.

Take a minute to consider your classroom, its physical properties, its decorations. The following survey will help you think about this important aspect of teaching that plays a major role in discipline.

Figure 3-1 Reflection: Evaluating Your Classroom

Select the appropriate answer(s) for each question.

1. The physical aspects of my classroom meet _____ .

_____ my needs   _____ my students' needs

_____ both my students' and my needs

2. I rearrange my room _____ .

_____ frequently   _____ each season

_____ once in a great while   _____ never

3. Young adolescents find my classroom _____ .

_____ inviting   _____ not sure

_____ uninviting

4. I display student work _____ .

_____ always   _____ sometimes

_____ never   _____ if I think it is worthy

_____ during parent teacher conferences

5. I rotate the posters and other display materials _____ .

_____ frequently   _____ when I feel like it

_____ every quarter   _____ every once in a while

_____ never   _____ after each project is completed

6. My classroom represents adolescent interests _____ .

_____ so much so that I took out a loan to pay for my purchases

_____ to the best of my knowledge   _____ not really

7. Three new things I did to my classroom last year were

_____ ,

_____ , and

_____ .

8. If I had unlimited resources, I would buy _____
for my classroom.

9. What I like best about my current classroom is

_____ .

10. Two things in my classroom I need to change first are

_____ and

_____ .

After completing the survey, answer these questions.

1. What are the strengths of my classroom?

2. What needs to be changed?

3. Is the classroom meeting the needs of young adolescents?

4. Is the classroom a sensory overload for some students?

5. How can I empower my students to help me with the change?

Seating arrangements

The arrangement of the furniture in a classroom is a critical consideration in classroom management. You need to figure out how to keep your students close to you. It is all about proximity. The farther away your students are, the harder it is to get to them. The farther away they are, the longer the obstacle course of backpacks and notebooks on the floor to get to them. Besides, if students are far away from you, how do you know whether they are working on the assignment or doing something totally unrelated to the class—maybe text messaging a friend? The farther away the students, the harder it is to make eye contact, observe, and monitor.

You might need to start from scratch. Take everything out of the room, including the teacher shrine (better known as the teacher

Figure 3-2 Seating in the Round

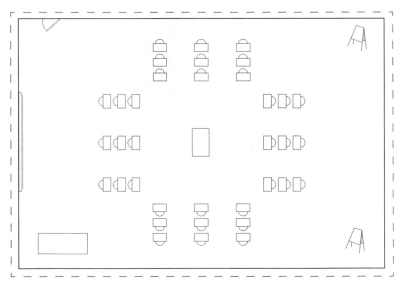

desk.) Then, making sure that no student's desk is more than three deep from you, fill in the room with your students' desks and other materials. One style is shown in Figure 3-2.

Figure 3-3 Classroom Seating Arrangements

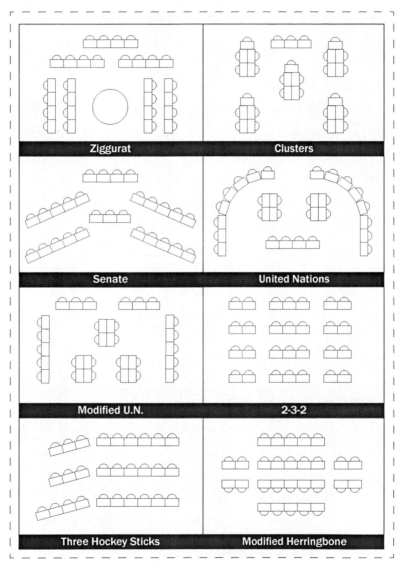

Be creative and unique. One teacher I know has two teacher desks around the room, and has a bar stool available for moving around the room as needed. Remember: if you and your students don't like it, you can change it in a couple of weeks. Figure 3-3 shows alternative seating arrangements that might help you develop the perfect classroom setting for your students.

Clean and tidy

Keeping the room clean and tidy is crucial. Students walking into a trashed room with paper all over the floor will first be reminded of their own bedrooms. Although they might feel right at home, we need to aim for a more clean and orderly environment. Meeting this goal is a difficult task the crazy last few minutes before the releasing of the bulls (better known as the ringing of the bell for students to change classes.) You, of course, must do your part to tidy up your parts of the room (prior to the start of each class is preferable.) Enlist students to help with watering plants, closing windows, washing chalkboards, and emptying pencil sharpeners. In elementary school they loved to do these things—and many middle school students still do.

Extreme classroom makeover

Although you may not have realized that your classroom does have a direct connection to classroom behavior and management, students' first impressions when they walk into a classroom form important assumptions. They notice everything, including how the room is arranged. If there are samples of student work on the walls or on the bulletin boards, students feel more ownership of the classroom. Young adolescents know and care how up-to-date the posters and other materials displayed are. Yes, this means you may have to take down your N'Sync poster, that cute "hang in there kitten" poster, and other outdated possessions. Discard the "READ" poster with yesterday's celebrities that young adolescents do not know. Be honest— some of the posters in your room cause you to wonder if the featured celebrity is still a star or even still alive.

Some classics, of course, are worth keeping such as the inflatable T-Rex, or the life-size cutout of you dressed in that unique spirit day outfit, or a strange saying or quotation that you use constantly. Such items deserve longevity.

One way to stay current with posters is to ask the manager of your local theater for posters of a popular (and appropriate— not R-rated) movie, which are typically removed after the movie has been in circulation for a month. The worst they can say is, "No," so why not ask? Be sure to tell the manager that you are a teacher. Also, check out your local thrift shops for posters and other materials that have historic value. Believe it or not, adolescents still know Elvis and a few 60s and 70s pop icons. Use your judgment about which icons are suitable for promotion as good models. Students will even respond to some of the old original classic posters, especially if there has been a recent remake of the movie. You will be surprised at how some of the posters in your room can be conversation starters, forging connections between you and your students, which will enable you to discern and then start to meet their needs. And even students having trouble getting interested in science may join in on an anticipatory- and surprisingly heavy-lesson about whether King Kong had real feelings and the true nature of animals.

Drugstores and the huge "box" stores are good sources of over-sized boxes, posters, and signs. Wallpaper books allow students to explore textures and designs for book covers, posters, backgrounds for bulletin boards, and tessellations for math. Check stores periodically for mismatched paints that they discard, and carpet squares or even pieces to wrap around desk legs with zip ties to muffle sound (stick-on chair leg pads also muffle sounds.)

Consider asking the PTA/PTO to provide funds for a classroom makeover. You can enlist faculty and parents in helping you and your students create an improved learning environment. Remember to get your principal's approval before you start and the parent liability forms signed prior to initiating any work. To make it a team or school-wide activity, run a contest and see what can happen with a little paint, creativity, and humor. Take into account guidelines (district policies) and stipulations (fire prevention regulations) to avoid having to dismantle a creation that covers an important piece of signage or is located too close to a vent. Don't be afraid to rework the entire room. Once a teacher found an old refrigerator door in a junk yard, cleaned it up, and mounted the door to a wall in his room. Students placed their favorite work on the door—an interesting and creative idea!

Student input and student focus

Take time to create a room that incorporates student input and reflects (appropriate) current pop culture. Young adolescents' tastes might change too quickly for us ever to keep up with the latest trend, but they do love it when we attempt to stay current. Have you ever noticed the shock and surprise of your students when you make a reference to current pop culture as you are teaching? Students look at you as though you are from another planet. Although they know that teachers are human beings with human needs, they are floored by evidence that we shop at Old Navy, eat at Chipotle, go see Twilight, watch reality TV, and even listen to MP3 players.

> "Make that strange piece of furniture Super-Glued to the floor with wax buildup an integral part of the classroom environment."

You can devote an area of the classroom to post bios of your students; samples of their achievements; and photos of them skiing, skateboarding, doing a craft, cheering at a game, attending a major sporting event; or just being a typical adolescent.

Another way to engage students is by hanging items such as wind socks, wind chimes, or streamers near the heating and cooling system—they make for a great visual display. When air comes out of the vents, the fluttering kites, swinging wind socks, and sounding wind chimes might distract some students, and fire regulations must be considered, but if your students can handle the movement and still concentrate, they will be intrigued by the display.

Try painting the ceiling tiles: You can take them out of the ceiling and have students paint an entire ceiling with murals. Or, you can put subject matter related to your content area on the tiles. Such things as a famous sayings, math equations, or science notations on the ceiling provide content to adolescents as they look up. For example, a science room might include the Periodic Table of the Elements or famous events in the history of science. Make sure that you follow your state's rules and remove all charts and other items as described in the rules for the state achievement tests.

If redesigning the whole room is a bit much, consider having a group of students design a section of your room and rotate the design group and the section of the room every couple of months. Think through when and how they will work most effectively and least invasively.

Creating a student-focused, safe place might cost a few dollars if it is to be vivid, creative, and interesting. However, young adolescents respect a place that is clean and visually exciting. Such a classroom sets the tone: it shows you know who they are, what their interests are, and that you care and respect them. They tend to behave better and learn more when they are respected and feel "known."

One middle school teacher fondly remembers a corner of her former classroom where students loved to read. It featured a leather sofa and some tall trees planted in large pots; it was a welcome, inviting respite in an otherwise busy environment. This teacher also used the lights to calm her students—the lights can raise the temperature ten degrees, and they don't always need to be on. During a recent conversation I had with a group of young adolescents, an eighth grade girl stated, "You can tell the personality of the teacher based on their (sic) classroom." An extremely insightful comment from a 15-year-old. You set the stage for learning by creating an environment that is truly adolescent-focused.

Those darn bulletin boards

Changing the bulletin boards can be tiresome, so why not let the students assume this responsibility? I always struggled with how to make the classroom bulletin boards engaging. I am not an artsy person—I struggle with drawing stick figures, and I cannot see how a huge square on the wall can be turned into a creative masterpiece. That is why I loved having willing and creative students. If you invite them to help, they can do amazing things to the room. Parents, too, like to help out, and this is one way they can stay involved in their kids' school lives; the assistance of students and parents should not be viewed as a way of helping a too-busy, dull teacher but as an opportunity to investigate a topic and practice some skills.

Bulletin board strategies

Ideas abound on the Web for using bulletin boards as tools for organization, classroom decoration, and even communicating recognition and discipline. Here are some basic ideas to help you create an inspiring and adolescent-friendly bulletin board.

- Offer students the opportunity to design meaningful bulletin boards. Let them take charge, be creative, and use their hidden talents to produce displays connected to the topic or unit under study.

- Empower students to help, to connect their personal interests to your subject, and to give them social interaction time with other adolescents as they work together.

- Ask local businesses for donations of oversized boxes and posters. Ask publishing companies for book jackets and cover proofs to display.

- Haunt bookstores for display materials they no longer want—these can be anything from stand-alone cardboard items to posters to items they had on shelves or hanging from the ceiling.

- Have students generate a timeline for updating and keeping them current.

- Students can come in early, stay late, or work during lunchtime depending on your availability to supervise them.

- Take photos of finished boards to help others generate ideas.

- Consider placing a "Giving Tree" outside your room with leaves that have items you need. You might be surprised to see how parents will take the leaves of requests and make purchases for you. Be courageous—put a new interactive whiteboard on the giving tree. You never know, someone might show up with one!

In addition to the content and design of your bulletin boards, think of ways to use them to improve the attractiveness and order of your classroom.

- Use old calendar pictures as backgrounds.
- Start simple and then build on your basic idea.
- Use for updates and information such as daily assignments and deadlines of upcoming projects.
- Daily post in a particular place the state content standard or essential question on which students will work.
- Use a calendar to list assignments for absent students.
- Designate a space to display accolades and awards for exceptional work.
- Display your most essential policies and procedures (no more than five) on signs. When you find yourself repeatedly responding, "Read the directions," you can simply point to the sign.
- Use for pre-teaching; display photos from magazines related to the upcoming unit; pose thought-provoking

questions about the photos that will draw upon students' preconceptions and misconceptions; ask students to write what they would like to know about the topic.

- Use the main board as a giant graphic organizer to show the relationships between the parts of the current unit students are studying. You can fill it out as you give an overview the first day and/or "build" it with them as you progress through the unit.

- Post strategies used throughout the year for processes such as working in the lab, what students should do when they run into an obstacle in reading comprehension, how to solve a particular type of problem, etc.

- Write vocabulary words from the chapter on one bulletin board—a word wall—and put a visual with each word. If there are comparative terms (exothermic, endothermic), color code the words linked to the exothermic with one color and those linked to endothermic another color.

- Extend learning using one of the bulletin boards as a resource or a reference point. Display captivating photographs and articles that relate to the content of the unit but for which time (and possibly standards coverage) will not allow.

- Use content-related cartoons to capture students' attention and further their thinking about a unit.

- Find a character to which young adolescents relate or find a comic or coloring book character that might appeal to them. Copy the picture, put it on the overhead projector, and project it onto the bulletin board and let the students color the board.

- Form a border around the room with book covers.

- Content and instruction are important, but so are the practical matters that enable sound teaching and learning. For proven best practices and frontline advice on managing the physical and emotional aspects of your environment, I recommend *Day One & Beyond* by Rick Wormeli (2003).

Questions for Reflection

1. In May if you asked some of your students about your bulletin boards of the past year, what would they say?

2. What are the main functions you want your bulletin boards to perform? How successfully have they served these functions?

3. What can you do to improve the boards' content while making them student-centered and engaging?

4. How does a classroom impact a students' success?

5. In what ways is your classroom a reflection of your teaching style?

chapter IV

Meet the Technology Challenge

Mr. Berckemeyer, why do you keep calling the computer a typewriter, and what is a ditto master?

When experienced middle level teachers compare this generation to past generations, they don't highlight differences in physical development from earlier times, but they do talk about how today's young adolescents think differently than the students of 10 years ago. Using technology, many multitask while carrying on three different conversations without saying a word. We try to understand their world as we struggle to remember the face-to-face conversation we had just 10 minutes ago with a parent or fellow teacher.

Another example of the technology generation gap is shown by our differing abilities to "see" the five or so different items on the television screen during cable news. While an anchor reports the news, a tape scrolls across the bottom of the screen with updates, a graphic sits over the anchor's shoulder, and a stock market ticker and the local weather report are on the right side of the screen. Many adults have difficulty focusing on one thing, let alone five. If you read the scrolling at the bottom, you miss the news or the weather report. However, a young adolescent can walk in the room, read the scrolling news report while listening to the reporter, then tell you the temperature and how your stocks are doing—all in less than 30 seconds.

Today's students' brains seem wired differently than those of past generations because

- They never need to look up a book in a card catalog—they can access just about anything with a few keystrokes (with the exception of intentionally blocked sites).
- Many have more capability of accessing information within seconds via their phones than they would find in any book in the school library.
- Their minds are moving and thinking at a different pace than our generation's.
- They demand faster rewards, answers, and information.
- They have been exposed to more information and data than past generations.

The challenge

Technology has become the young adolescent's closest friend, but at what cost? I recall watching a young adolescent playing a game on his handheld Game Boy in an airport. Meanwhile, his parents were talking about lost luggage and other frustrations of travel with total strangers. He was so engrossed in the moment of capturing a fortress or taking over a lost kingdom that he missed some valuable modeling of communicating and interacting with others. However, he was likely gaining creativity and other talents using the technology; after all, why should he care about the luggage or his parents' conversations? Is the use of technology taking away from the family core? Are there dinner conversations about family members' activities anymore?

This is a challenge for today's teachers: How can we help students develop technology skills of the 21st century while meeting the need for conversation and face-to-face interaction? Because we are so accustomed to interacting face-to-face or via phone conversations, we become easily frustrated when adolescents are so absorbed in their electronics that they fail to see us or engage with us in a live conversation.

Technology is consuming this generation. They crave immediate responses, seek multiple answers, dialogue to solve problems, text, search the Web, and literally let their fingers do the walking and the talking. What communication skills will adolescents have 10 to 20 years from now? Will they go to school online and never talk with another person (non-virtually) unless, perhaps, by accident? If so, we must place more priority on developing adolescents' social skills by continuing to use cooperative learning groups and encouraging students to interact in school. This may mean students will need more time for talking during class to develop face-to-face social skills.

Cooperative use of technology

E-mail, audio and video chats, iMing, Skype, etc., provide great opportunities for motivating students to learn by taking advantage of young adolescents' desire to work with others. By using digital technology, young adolescents can now connect to many more people in many more parts of the world than young adolescents of previous generations.

Note all the words indicating development of social skills in the ISTE (International Society for Technology in Education) student standard for communication and collaboration (http://tiny.cc/ISTE) that follows.

> Students use digital media and environments to communicate and work collaboratively, including at a distance, to support individual learning and contribute to the learning of others. Students
>
> a. Interact, collaborate, and publish with peers, experts, or others employing a variety of digital environments and media.
>
> b. Communicate information and ideas effectively to multiple audiences using a variety of media and formats.
>
> c. Develop cultural understanding and global awareness by engaging with learners of other cultures.

d. Contribute to project teams to produce original works or
    solve problems.

For those who worry that courtesy and socialization are dimin-
ished as time spent on technology increases, look to the findings
of the Maine Learning Technology Initiative (MLTI), in which
educators worried that socialization would suffer with the
advent of the laptops, but found the opposite was true. Jill
Spencer, an educational consultant with over 30 years' experience teaching middle school, says of the initiative:

> Students collaborate more, share their work, give feedback, and
> potentially learn to interact with folks all over the world—up
> close and personal, with tools like Skype. Student blogs and
> websites give them voice like they have never had before. I was
> recently in an art class where the kids were working on a graphic
> design project—they were sending their work to students across
> the room to get feedback—all via their laptops. They were on task
> and engaged in revision. The teacher had trained them how to do
> this and how to give feedback. It's all about good teaching. Again,
> if the curriculum and instruction is inline with *This We Believe*,
> students will be working collaboratively on projects that have
> unbelievable resources and multiple tools for demonstrating their
> knowledge—the students are always helping each other figure out
> how something works and then showing the teacher how to do it.

Part of our preparing middle school students for a global econo-
my is to teach them digital courtesy and the difference between
face-to-face communication and digital communication. Also,

they must learn how easy it is to be misunderstood when communicating online because of the lack of facial clues, tone of voice, and lack of gestures.

Educating and holding students accountable for school technology policy

Learning to make good choices about how, when, and why they use technology is a critical skill for students. Students need to learn to respect others' rights to privacy; understand boundaries; and accept accountability for stealing others' data, movies, or music, and for violating laws protecting individuals. They need to know what options, rules, and etiquette are appropriate for the different forms of technologies. They need to understand that the technology itself is neither good nor bad but that there is a need for balancing the use of technology in their lives. The cumulative effect of always being in digital communication through such things as their phones, computers, and iPods can deprive them of important stimuli from other parts of the world and from live personal interactions that can be both rewarding and skill building.

Technology diary activity

 One way to raise students' awareness of the impact of technology is to have them keep a technology diary for one week. Students record their use of all technology including surfing the Web, talking on their cell phones, listening to their iPods, and all other forms of technology that they use at home, at school, and everywhere else. Students should record their location, the length of time they used the technology, in what capacity they used it, and what else (if anything) they were doing at the time.

Figure 4-1 shows a sample data table for the activity. After students compile the information, have them analyze it by identifying trends, determining where they use technology most, and whether they think about how their using the technology affects others. As an extension, students could challenge themselves to not use any digital technology for a day or an entire week and encourage their families to refrain from doing so as well. A class discussion on the positive and negative results of the "digital fast" would further enlighten students.

Figure 4-1 Technology Diary

Technology	Location	Time of Day	How long	Purpose	Other Activities
Cell phone					
Computer					
Ipod					

Digital citizenship

The ISTE digital citizenship standard is

Students understand human, cultural, and societal issues related to technology and practice legal and ethical behavior. Students:

a. Advocate and practice safe, legal, and responsible use of information and technology.

b. Exhibit a positive attitude toward using technology that supports collaboration, learning, and productivity.

c. Demonstrate personal responsibility for lifelong learning.

d. Exhibit leadership for digital citizenship.

Here are a few websites with useful information:

http://www.commonsense.com/internet-safety-guide/

http://coe.ksu.edu/digitalcitizenship/index.htm

http://www.livinginternet.com/i/ia_nq.htm

Many districts have an acceptable use policy (AUP), which must be followed. Most include the prohibition of

- Cell phone ringers turned on during class.

- Instant messaging during class.

- Playing games on laptops or handheld computers during class.

- Accessing pornographic websites in school.

- Using websites, e-mail, or cell phones to bully other students.

- Using instant messaging and e-mail shorthand for class work.

- Using online data or information without crediting the source.

Degradation of grammar and spelling

What can we do about the degradation of grammar and spelling due to texting, chatrooms, Facebook, and My Space? Teach students that there is a time for informal, "texting" language and a time for formal, standard English and maintain high standards for their writing in class.

Phone policy

Many schools and teachers have established cell phone policies that make controlling phone interruptions easier. However, the use of cell phones by students in schools is a much more complex issue. Some parents do not support school policies of

"Students love when you talk doctor visits on your phone— don't be surprised if they tell you they are sorry you have a rash."

restricting phone usage and immediately return confiscated phones to students. Often, it is difficult to track down and discipline students using their phones for sexting, or sending messages or pictures of a sexual nature. Once the messages and pictures are sent, they turn up everywhere. Widely distributed, they can result in charges of child pornography, youths forever registered as sexual offenders, and lawsuits against teachers and administrators.

If cell phones are allowed in your school, remember to turn off your own cell phone to model the importance of class time and show that the rules apply to everyone. If all students have access to phones with cameras, have students use their phones as a learning tool when lessons would be enhanced with a camera, illustrating projects, texting answers, and doing research.

Using technology with purpose

Before using any type of technology in the classroom, research it thoroughly and have a specific purpose that you can state clearly for students. Focus on acceptable use as well as restricted use.

- Have multiple things going on in various areas of the room. Use two overheads in separate parts of the room; run scrolling text "updates" as you give instructions.

- Use and have students create their own iMovies, podcasts, and interactive whiteboard presentations to convey content and lessons.

- Take technology classes or find other ways to stay current with the latest digital devices and programs.

- If your students have technology, create homework lessons that require using cell phones or the Internet.

- Investigate how your students are using instant messaging to do homework and school projects. Are there specific issues that you need to address?

- Have students use wikis to create collaborative projects; once information is posted, it can be updated and expanded, and it provides documentation of who modified the project, when, and how. Glossaries, study guides, supporting documents, and much more can be available to students and parents anytime on the Web.

- Have students use instant messaging and blogs to support the classroom content as they share information and their creativity with others.

- Use blogs and wikis to share classroom activities and events with parents; establish and communicate a frequency for posting. Communicate rules for posting (no profanity, no flaming (hostile and insulting interaction between Internet users), no bullying).

- Use classroom management software to post all assignments and to contact parents.

- Use electronic communication tools to format and share your team's units, to communicate extra credit assignments, to send a monthly parent newsletter from the team, and to store worksheets and team e-mails.

Wikipedia

Although many people do not see value in Wikipedia because it is not a scholarly publication, Jill Spencer sees it as a great tool for students to use for generating questions and getting an overview of a topic.

> It can be used in an exploratory method for teaching students how to evaluate the different entries and increasing their information literacy/fluency as part of a comprehensive plan across grades and subjects. A great strategy would be for the kids to create an entry for Wikipedia and be part of the process. In this way, use digital tools to engage and challenge students; don't try to convince students the technology isn't as good as print material. Also, Wikipedia has different levels sorted by reading ability—it may be a great resource for students with reading issues. They can get started with the entry and then expand their search. Too often, kids with reading problems get very frustrated searching the Web because a lot of material is written for adults.
>
> From an e-mail May 19, 2009

Laptop use

Encourage students to use laptops if they are available, permitted by your school, and can be used securely. The Maine Learning Technology Initiative (MLTI) has had a 1:1 laptop initiative since 2002, in which 40,000 students and 6,000 teachers participated. The initiative shows that one laptop for one student works: it provides equity of resources, and the key to its success is educators who know how to integrate technology into their daily practices. Check out the MLTI website for useful information at http://www.maine.gov/mlti/index.shtml. Based on what she learned with the introduction of laptops in Maine, Jill Spencer offers these tips.

- If kids are engaged in challenging work that they find relevant, they stay on task—even with the temptation of games just a click away. Edutopia has a great site on project-based learning (http://www.edutopia.org/project-learning). Skowhegan Regional Middle School offers an example of this type of learning from the Maine initiative (http://www.msad54.org/sams/integration/index.shtml).

- Procedures, procedures, procedures! Teachers who take the time to train students on the use and care of their laptops and take time to anticipate potential trouble spots rarely have issues.

  1. Room organization: the room cannot be arranged with the teacher up front facing rows of students and the backs of laptops. Instead, try U-shape, small groups, or other arrangements that allow the teacher to easily see each student's screen.

2. When you need students' undivided attention, use simple cues such as "Lids down."

3. Teach kids what to do when the laptop battery runs low and when other common glitches occur.

4. Teach kids when to have their airport on and when to have it off.

5. Have acceptable use contracts in place that state appropriate consequences for the breaking of rules. Taking the laptop away is not the right thing to do—we don't take kids' pencils and pens away if they write a note; we don't take their textbook away if they write in it. The laptop is a learning tool like anything else we use in school. School leadership has to be on board with the policies that make sense.

From an e-mail May 19, 2009

The Facebook issue

If your district permits teachers to create their own Facebook and MySpace accounts, initiate a faculty discussion about balancing the risks and benefits. If you do decide to go on Facebook, do not post photos that would offend the most conservative member of the school board, and do not say stupid stuff. Many teachers agree that "friending" students is not appropriate due to the lack of control about what is posted, and it could send a wrong message about the relationships between teachers and students.

Students aren't your friends, they are your students. People can write anything on your wall and can "tag" pictures with your name, which then appear in your profile, so you do not have 100 % control over what current or former students might see. You might consider having a "class Facebook" with very specific and limited uses. Some districts encourage teachers to have Facebook accounts, and some even require it; some teachers are comfortable with managing the risks of its use and think the benefits outweigh the risks.

Although new teachers may not immediately understand why they should not befriend students, they will likely find out through experience that even though some practices may be legal, they are not wise. Teachers' professional and personal lives overlap, but regardless of the setting, people still hold teachers to a high standard of behavior.

As an alternative, you could set up a class wiki as a discussion board or as a place for kids to post pictures of pets or hobbies (like an electronic bulletin board). On a wiki, you can control everything that is posted. Put your lessons and homework assignments on the page. Record an awesome video of you snowboarding or skiing—students are always shocked to find that you have outside hobbies.

Technology safety

Teaching students the risks of technology is key; young adolescents do not always understand the possible outcomes of their behavior. Neil Sandham, a teacher from Airdrie, Alberta, reported he had heard of eighth grade girls using their cell phones to set up meetings with grade 6 boys; they would meet in the bathrooms, have sex, film it, and post it on their social websites. And yet, some parents object to the school interfering with the students' use of phones (their children's private property).

Helpful hints for teachers regarding technology:

- Do not use your personal cell phone in class. Never answer a call during teaching time—not only is it rude and unprofessional, it sets a bad example and sends the message that there is a double standard for following school rules. Besides, students can hear your conversation. Listening to your personal conversations is one way they find out embarrassing things about you. They love it when you talk doctor visits on your phone. They might even tell you they are sorry you have a rash—all thanks to your lack of discretion. Also avoid working on e-mail during class—again, very unprofessional.

- Check all websites before making them part of student assignments.

- Follow your district's guidelines for vetting the videos you show in class.

- If you currently have a Facebook account or any other website, delete anything to which students should not have access. Pay attention, new teachers! Delete the photo of you in college celebrating your football team's victory and have your friends with links to your site do the same. If there is a photo of you being a typical college student, adolescents will find it, so delete the photo of you in front of the beer can pyramid.

- Give parents a copy of the district's acceptable use policy and refer to it occasionally when communicating digitally with parents as a group.

- Read *The Rebooting of a Teacher's Mind* by Brenda Dyck (2004), an essential teacher resource with dozens of websites packed with practical advice, hints, teaching and classroom management strategies, and professional development guidance.

Impact of social networks on students

ChildrenOnline.org, an Internet safety organization, lists 10 concerns with students using Facebook and other social networks such as YouTube, MySpace, Hi5, Friendster, Xanga, DeviantArt, and others.

Figure 4-2 Concerns about Facebook

1. For those schools that allow it, the use of Facebook in our communities can take an inordinate amount of Internet bandwidth.

2. Using Facebook takes time. Often, a LOT of time! Young adolescents have an irresistible urge to interact with their peers, and, often, they have unlimited digital access; this can lead to their use of social networking sites becoming all-consuming.

3. Using Facebook can give a false sense of privacy. In addition, a feeling of anonymity and lack of social responsibility can develop from using text-centered telecommunications—which results in students posting embarrassing, humiliating, denigrating, and hurtful content in text, photos, and videos. They need to learn that nothing is private online; they need to see examples of serious consequences that can occur.

   "Perhaps the most common reason that teens' private information is exposed is that they are easily tricked into accepting friend requests from strangers. ... Teens accept as friends 44%–87% of the strangers knocking on their doors in Facebook."

4. There are thousands of scams targeting teens in their social networks, especially Facebook and MySpace.

5. Spyware and Adware installations are very serious concerns.

6. We need to acknowledge that screens act as a moral disconnect for many of our students. Increasingly, young adolescents are socializing in a world without caring adults watching out for them, setting expectations, and overseeing the setting of boundaries.

7. Our students have very little knowledge about how much they are being marketed to; how their purchasing decisions and attitudes are being manipulated; how their personal information is being used; and even how valuable that personal information is.

8. Research shows that teens are increasingly using telecommunications.

9. Children are increasingly turning to making friendships and building relationships online. Children are far too inexperienced in social skills to use telecommunications tools to build relationships in a healthy and safe manner online.

10. The meaning of the word "friend" is changing for our students, and this change puts them at risk in several ways. Some of their Facebook "friends" are complete strangers; we need to talk with them about the typical values of friendship (trust, love, support, sharing). http://www.nais.org/resources/article.cfm?ItemNumber=151505

Doug Fodeman and Marje Monroe, Co-Directors of ChildrenOnline.org

Please understand that I know everyone has their own level of comfort regarding technology. Using technology affects your teaching styles and your personal beliefs. However, because students truly embrace technology, we need to understand how to manage it and how to use it effectively in our classrooms. As Jill Spencer says,

Accept the fact that the kids will always know more than you do about the digital world. Embrace the fact and learn from and with your students. Design units that push everyone's thinking and experiment with Web 2.0 and other digital tools!

Questions for Reflection

1. What is one goal for using technology to improve your teaching that you can realistically meet this year? What information and supports will you need to accomplish this?

2. With what current issues about technology safety do your students need the most information and help?

3. On what technology projects could your students work cooperatively to improve their social skills while learning necessary content?

4. What are the most pressing concerns of your staff in terms of technology training?

5. What technology issues does your school need to address with parents and guardians?

chapter V

Teach Social Skills and Manners

Mr. Berckemeyer, I can burp the Star Spangled Banner.

While technology has and will continue to empower our youth, it has also resulted in a shift in manners. Have you ever been standing in line at the grocery store and had an adolescent walk right in front of you without saying "Excuse me"? When this happens, you think, "I cannot believe parents raise their children the way they do. How rude!" But stop and think about it for a moment. If most of adolescents' interactions are not face-to-face with live people, they might be unfamiliar with and unpracticed in using common courtesy. This is teachable and is something we can enforce in our classrooms and schools.

Explain that using manners allows people to live together without embarrassing themselves and each other. Here are some examples of how to deal with courtesy issues.

- Model the practices yourself: say "Hello," "Please," and "Thank you" to students.

- Greet students every day as they enter your room.

- Reinforce the language you want students to use: when you hear, "She is a XXXXX", translate it to "She is having a difficult day."

- Acknowledge students who do charity work and good deeds inside and outside school.

- Reward Citizens of the Month by giving them fast food coupons, announcing their names on the public address system, putting their pictures and names on the bulletin board and in the school newsletter, or awarding them wooden plaques.

- Be honest with students. Talk to them about appropriate social behaviors.

- Pick your battles. Because you cannot address every rudeness, focus on those that interrupt learning and those that are personally vicious.

- Develop a school-wide, classroom, or team policy on courtesy. Post the rules in hallways and rooms.

- Discuss the topic at a faculty meeting. Generate ideas for encouraging basic manners.

- Host a formal dinner party to show young adolescents how to use manners. Do this right before you take them to the theater, a large social gathering, or on a field trip.

- Treat your students with respect and make sure they treat you the same. Early in the year, as you talk through the classroom policies and procedures, emphasize that the school is focused on helping students gain strength in a positive, collaborative way rather than from put-down interactions, such as doing the dozens, that may be a neighborhood routine for showing strength.

- Do not let them call you just by your title ("Ms." Or "Hey, Mr."). Ask them to use your full last name.

- Stop kids when they push others or bump into someone, and instruct them to use an appropriate apology.

- Teach them that when a conflict with someone is over, they need to shake hands and apologize.

"Remember, if you don't A.S.K, you don't G.E.T."

Every educator wants students to be polite, punctual, and proper. However, with adolescents that may not always be possible. Part of growing up is to break some of the traditions handed down by adults. Adolescents naturally push buttons and experiment with rude behaviors. However, with some correcting, monitoring, and role modeling they will figure out the proper way to act. It just takes time and consistency. We are there unconditionally every day: we wait for them, we greet them, and we provide a safe environment for them. Adolescents want to be secure and respected—we just need to let them know that it all starts with practicing common courtesy, which shows we respect and care about other people. Adolescents like a teacher

who is a little strict and has good classroom management skills.
If you model it, they WILL aspire to it!

Bullying

Most schools have a zero-tolerance policy regarding bullying, a
big problem in the United States. Data from a national survey
of students in grades 6-10 (Nansel et al., 2001) show that about
30% are involved in bullying, either as a bully, the target of a
bully or both. A safe school is a long-term goal and requires daily
effort to reinforce the school community's values. As a teacher,
you are on the front line daily in courageously confronting
inappropriate behavior. First, identify the inappropriate
behavior; next ask the bully what he or she wanted or needed;
then help the bully identify alternative responses that would
have been appropriate. If the infraction warrants, refer the bully
to the administration. Some schools have boxes for students to
report bullying confidentially so that students who fear reprisals
if caught talking with staff have more opportunities to participate in creating a safe school community.

The parent piece of the puzzle

Ideally, students come to you after years of practicing common
courtesy toward their peers and elders, but let's say, by chance,
you don't have such a roster of students. One way to reinforce
the practicing of respectful behaviors is to communicate to your
students' parents and guardians the expectations you have for
student behavior in your class. You might point out to parents
that knowing and practicing appropriate social behaviors is a
key factors in students' eventual successful graduation from

high school. At the beginning of the school year, send a letter to parents describing your expectations, the supplies students will need for your classes, and your phone number and e-mail address. Once parents and their young adolescent discuss it, students can bring in the parent- and student-signed letter for bonus points. File this form in case the parents and/or teen later claim they were not informed of the expectations.

Parent power

Young adolescents crave power and seek it both at home and at school. Anyone who has raised a young adolescent knows that the mood of a young adolescent can dictate the mood of an entire house. As a teacher, you can also witness how power can affect a family. How many times have you heard a parent say, "I don't know what to do with her"? You are thinking, "She is 12; how can you have given your power to a 12-year-old?" When it happens, it can frustrate parents, teachers, and the student as well.

Most parents want to do a good job of parenting. The following suggestions in Figure 5-1 can be shared with parents on a website or in a newsletter.

Figure 5-1 Suggestions for parents

How to Raise an Adolescent without Going Crazy

- Be consistent. 10:00 p.m. means 10:00 p.m.—no exceptions. The more consistent you are, the easier it is for the young adolescent to live up to your expectations.

- Teach them to say, "I feel..., I need..., I want..."

- Check up on them. Don't hesitate to call to make sure they went where they said they were going.

- Don't take it personally. The mood of your son or daughter should not dictate the mood of the entire house. Wait a few minutes and the child's mood will change.

- Keep the school backpack cleaned out; a weekly cleaning will turn up missing assignments, notices of upcoming important school events, and dirty Tupperware ™ with moldy science projects in it.

- Talk with other parents and form your own support system; find out what methods they are using effectively.

- Use the school schedule as the basis for making a personal planner for your child; add important extracurricular activities and family commitments.

- Enjoy their humor. The middle school years can be a fun time for adolescents as their senses of humor develop; don't be afraid to laugh with them.

- Be aware of technology use; it is critically important to help your child learn the appropriate uses and dangers of their digital world.

Figure 5-1 Suggestions for parents (continued)

- Keep in touch with the school—remember there are always two sides to a story. Talk to the teacher and get his or her input before rushing to judgment.
- And, finally, remember that you are the parent.

Without a doubt, parents will be challenged by interacting daily with their developing adolescent. You and the parents need to support each other as much as possible. Some parents are frightened of the school and teachers, and some are suspicious; perhaps they had bad experiences in school, or they may speak little or no English. Parents sometimes are defensive and withdraw if they do not feel safe in relating to the teacher and school. Identifying any barriers and breaking them down is key to students' success, as research shows students with involved parents (regardless of socioeconomic background) achieve success and go on to postsecondary education.

I know that sometimes getting even a few parents to show up at meetings can be challenging, but for those parents who seek information, the following tips from Judith Baenen, a former middle school teacher and administrator, will help them better communicate with their children.

Figure 5-2 Parent Information

Tips for Living Successfully with Your Young Adolescent

Think ahead. One of the best tips for parents is "be prepared." As your son or daughter enters the middle school years, get ready for at least occasional conflicts. Think through what is truly important to you. Is the hairstyle as important as the homework? Isn't curfew more of a concern than crabbiness? Obviously, dawdling is a lot easier to accept than drugs. As these give-and-take situations start, know ahead of time which areas you are willing to negotiate and which areas are absolute.

Break down big chores into small parts. Sometimes young people feel overwhelmed by tasks, especially those they've let go for a long time. A disastrous bedroom, 23 overdue math assignments, a long-term project that's "suddenly" due in a few days (or hours!)—all of these can lead a young adolescent to give up rather than get started.

Help your child by setting up smaller goals. Clean off your bed; get five assignments done tonight; assemble the materials for the project. Young adolescents have trouble structuring tasks so that they are more approachable. We can help them in this.

Encourage your middle schooler to keep a daily to-do list (weekly is too much). You may need to assign a specific time to each task. When the task is completed, the student draws a line through it.

Figure 5-2 Parent Information (continued)

**Remind your middle schooler about appointments and due
dates.** Think ahead about materials required for a project (unless you look forward to late-evening visits to the store). This
will not last forever. When this same child was learning to walk,
we held her hands and made the path smooth. Now she is learning to take on a tremendous assortment of life tasks and changes;
hand-holding (but not the firm, physical grip previously necessary) is needed for about a year or so as your middle schooler
gets started on the road to being a responsible adult.

Be willing to listen—but don't poke or pry. Kids this age value
independence and often seem secretive. Keeping to themselves is
part of the separateness they are trying to create. Let them know
you'd love to help them, but don't push them into a defensive
position.

**If your child is in the midst of a longtime friendship that is
falling apart, the best thing you can do is stand by and be a
good listener.** It is devastating for us to see our children hurt-
ing, but taking sides or intervening is not appropriate, nor will it
help. Young adolescents do survive these hurts, especially if they
know we are there to listen to their pain.

Accept them for who they are. Listen; don't needlessly criti-
cize; back them up when they're right; and pick them up when
they're down.

Help them gain perspective. Young adolescents need to learn that
being "best friends" isn't always smooth sailing. People have differences of opinion and even get angry with one another, but they still

Figure 5-2 Parent Information (continued)

care for each other. When kids are involved in those "I-hate-her-she-is-so-stuck-up" and "How-could-she-do-this-to-me" conversations, parents must help them see that one problem need not ruin a relationship, but stubbornness might. Middle schoolers have a lot of spats and falling outs, but, often, the friends are back together in a short time.

When reprimanding, deal only with the precise problem, don't bring in other issues. "The trash is still here, and I want it out, now," is better than, "You are so lazy! I told you to take the trash out two hours ago, and it's still here! You'd live in a pigsty, wouldn't you? Well, you aren't the only one in this house, you know..."

If the issue is minor, keep things light. The shoes on the floor, the wet towel on the bed, the carton left open—these are maddening, perhaps, but not earth-shattering. Call attention to them in a humorous way so that your middle schooler knows you want action but you aren't being punitive. "Either the cat's smarter than I thought, or you left the milk carton open on the counter. One of you please put it back before it spoils."

Don't' use power unless it's urgent. Parents have the ultimate power, and kids know it. We don't have to "prove" it to them at every turn. Save your strength for those really important issues you've decided are non-negotiable. Eventually, kids are going to possess power of their own, and we want them to be able to use it wisely.

Based on *H.E.L.P. How to Enjoy Living with a Preadolescent* by Judith Baenen

Questions for Reflection

1. How would you rate your school's "climate of civility?" What issues do the faculty and administration need to address?

2. What can you personally do to increase your effectiveness as a role model for mannerly, courteous behavior?

3. For one day, keep a record of how many times you ignore inappropriate behaviors in your class and in the hallways.

4. Identify ways you can increase parents' knowledge of raising an adolescent.

5. Name the reward systems you use to thank students for politeness and respectfulness.

chapter VI

Channel Adolescent Power

Mr. Berckemeyer, I will not sit down, and you can't make me!

This chapter discusses the two sides of student power; they sometimes seem driven to use it in negative ways but then amaze us with their capacity for empathy and helpfulness toward others. I will delve into issues of procrastination, suggest a unique strategy for holding students accountable for class work, and provide a lesson in empowering students to make choices and work at their own paces.

Negative power plays

Children of all ages struggle with power issues, and power plays are a factor throughout a young adolescent's life. Have you ever thought, "Middle school students can be the meanest and cruelest people on the face of the earth"? They can kick a friend's backpack all the way down the hall while calling her an inappropriate name. Feeling guilty, they drop a dollar in the bucket for a world disaster relief effort, and suddenly all the guilt is gone.

Examples of negative student power plays:

- Procrastinating: They exercise their power as they take as much time as possible to complete a two-minute activity.

- Wandering around and looking for something to do or someone to bother

- Tapping or hitting someone with a pencil, ruler, or any available object

- Acting like they did not hear the question

- Making the famous "I don't get it" statement

- Rolling the eyes

- Pushing someone or something

- Constantly looking disgusted—the rolled-up nose and wrinkly forehead (which will result in horrible lines when they are older)

- Using confrontational looks or gestures

- Using inappropriate language

- Swinging of the arms toward others

- Making derogatory remarks

- Having an "I don't care" attitude ("Whatever")

Handling procrastination

First, let's discuss the power play of procrastination. How to deal with student procrastination is the million-dollar question because it is usually passive and not as "in your face" as other power plays. Young adolescents have mastered the art of drawing out a 10-minute lesson into a week's worth of work. Here are some typical ways adolescents avoid working and some ideas and strategies you might want to try.

Work avoidance methods:

- The "stealth method" is the most common tactic used by young adolescents. A young adolescent scans the room while pretending to work. The student is, however, focusing in on the next target—usually a friend or someone who everyone routinely picks on. When the selected target walks by, the student pokes or kicks the target or makes a mean comment hoping to coax an eruption from the other person.

- Other classic procrastination methods include staring at the pencil to see if it has grown in the last several minutes, the "Oops, I dropped my piece of paper again," sharpening of pencils, using a hall pass to roam the halls, asking questions to get the teacher's attention, and introducing a topic that gets the teacher off task.

Strategies for managing procrastination include the following:

- The teacher plays a critical role in the pacing and motivation of students. If you want kids to work, you have to work the room. Pretend it is the cocktail party you never get invited to because you are too busy sleeping or grading papers on the weekends. Mingle! Walk around and greet everyone. Participate in small talk with your young adolescents. Pretend you own the room—after all, you really do! This allows you to make sure work is being done.

- If students are not working, tell them you are not letting them leave until they finish the first set of questions. Then make sure you hold them accountable.

- At the beginning of class, give students only half of the worksheet; later give them the other half. This strategy counters the tendency of students to look at the time in a class period and the number of questions and feel, "I will never finish this in time." For some students that list of twenty questions is overwhelming, and they shut down before they even start. Breaking the assignment into smaller sections helps them gain skills in pacing themselves, problem solving, and test taking—all of which build confidence and self-esteem while challenging their defeatist attitudes.

- Occasionally tell them the first half are for a grade and the last half are for bonus points; it is amazing how many want that extra credit.

- Have you ever noticed that when you are energized and ready to go, your students' attitude and motivation will follow? Don't hesitate to tell your students there is so much to do today that they have to keep moving quickly.

Remember, many of them are comfortable multitasking with electronics and seeing several pieces of information at once. Once you get their attention, you can then break things down into smaller pieces.

- Start class by saying, "We have a million things to do today." Write on the board a list of 10 items that students need to complete by the end of the day, and don't worry about overwhelming them. Here is the important part: of the list of 10 items, only 5 are real. Your students will never know that some of the assignments are fake. They have no idea that "Reflection Sheet A97.2" does not exist. Then, as the students behave and start to work, erase some of the fake assignments, telling them it is a reward for behaving.

- Put trays of papers in the back of the room for students to pick up their handouts or their graded work when they enter the room. This prevents them from taking forever to pass papers in or distribute them.

Holding students accountable for their work

Adolescents expect to be allowed to leave the classroom when the bell rings. Unless the class is right before lunch or electives when a teacher could keep students past the bell to complete assignments, students can usually transition to their next class whether or not they have completed their work. However, holding your students accountable is critical to their future success.

Let me share a story with you. I once had a lazy, procrastinating student who did not complete his work—in fact, he would not even put a heading on the paper, although he was fully capable of completing the assignment. My teammates and I discussed this student and decided that, after the bell rang, he would remain in language arts class to finish his work. The student ended up staying in that class all day, and much to my shock, he still had done nothing by the end of the day. But here is the amazing part: I met him at his bus first thing the following morning, and he came in and finished the assignment within five minutes.

Pleased with this success, I optimistically tried the approach with another student. The outcome was the same: he finished his work. Interestingly, after sitting in the class for three periods, he began to answer the questions before any of the other students had a chance to respond. After hearing the same lesson three

"Sometimes letting go of the classroom and empowering students is the best thing to do. However, it can cause angst and frustration for the teacher. Young adolescents will seek power any way they can—the question becomes 'do you want to facilitate the process or let them control the process?!"

times that day, the message sank in, and he became the brightest kid in the class. Of course, students eventually figured out the system and used it to avoid attending classes they didn't like and to disrupt the other classes taking place when they were held back.

Before using this tactic, make sure you cover all the bases. Discuss the tough, practical issues regarding this process with your teammates and determine on a case-by-case basis which students this strategy would help most. Start small, and then build on your success.

Before holding back a student in class, some of the questions your team can consider are:

1. Why is the student not doing the work? Is it because the level is too high or is the student just lazy? Is there an emotional reason such as trouble at home or with another student, or is there another reason for acting out?

2. How will the student make up missed work from the other core classes?

3. What will be the impact on electives or exploratory classes? For which students will this process work? For which will it not work?

4. How do we evaluate the process to see if it is working?

5. Do we do this with a small group of students or the whole group?

6. How do we involve parents and administrators?

Student empowering activity

This activity is an example of how to increase students' motivation and participation by allowing them to make choices and decisions. The activity is a perfect review lesson for any subject area.

Teacher background: Tell your students each of them need to accumulate 60 points within the class period. Students will choose their assignments, each having a different point value—they can do any combination of activities as long as they add up to 60 points. A basic sample activity using language arts materials follows.

Figure 6-1 Language Arts Sample Activity

REVIEW ACTIVITY

Directions: Read the short story Why Ants Burn So Quickly. Then choose and complete activities from the list below to equal 60 points.

- Answer the five questions at the end of the short story. Point value: 25

- Review the list of vocabulary on page 49 of your language arts text. Define the vocabulary and use each word in a sentence that relates to school. Point value: 20

- Create a menu using the information from the story *Why Ants Burn So Quickly.* Be creative with your menu items. Point value: 20

Figure 6-1 Language Arts Sample Activity

- Write a short story about the life of an ant. Use a main character, conflict, and resolution in your short story. Point value: 40

- Using the Internet, research information on ants. Point value: 5 for each reference; limit 20 points

- List 10 reasons why people hate ants. Point value: 5

- Write a well-developed fiction or nonfiction paragraph on how ants help humans. Point value: 10

In this particular activity, the teacher could give students extra points for submitting drafts of their writing or their proofreading. As you can see, the list of possible assignments is endless. Assign the activities requiring more time, creativity, thought, and detail the highest point values. Students get to choose their work based on their abilities, skills, and natural interests (guide students who typically don't challenge themselves) while reviewing content.

Using their power for good

Young adolescents can also be the most kind, giving, and compassionate people on the face of the earth. They collect canned goods to feed the hungry and volunteer to run clothing drives for the homeless. Helping whenever there is a major injustice in the world, they feel sorrow and pain for the less fortunate.

Some young adolescents are more responsible than some adults. Given opportunities, adolescents make positive change in their school, community, and world.

Adolescents have done some great things:

- After hurricane Katrina, a 13-year-old young adolescent formed a group called the Mowrons to help mow the grass in the local parks of New Orleans.
- In Florida a young adolescent saved a drowning man.
- Middle school students have raised hundred of thousands of dollars for needy families, local libraries, and for world disaster relief.
- Young adolescents have been responsible for painting murals over graffiti in urban areas.
- They have planted gardens in inner cities.
- They have bought playground equipment for elementary schools.
- They have walked, run, bowled, danced, and sung to raise money for local charities.
- They have posted personal videos on Web chat spaces denouncing school violence including gun violence, beatings, and teacher bashing.

It is easy to help people you don't know; helping someone you do know takes maturity and conviction. Some young adolescents focus their power against the weak in their schools. They mock the student with the ugly coat or the wrong type of shoes or shirt. And heaven forbid another student shows emotion by having a bit of a breakdown in front of others. Young adolescents' strong desire to pounce on that weaker child for showing emotion and to embarrass or harass another student is all about power. If a student courageously helps another student who is powerless, the helping student often becomes a target as well, hearing comments such as, "How can you help her? Why are you being nice to that freak? Is he your new best friend?" Our job as educators is to teach that power comes not only from helping people we do not know but also from helping others around us. Here are suggestions for ways students can be honored and supported in their own schools.

- Have students nominate a Student of the Week. Each week change the criteria so that young adolescents must look for the attributes in students other than those most popular. Teachers can make nominations, too.

- Reinforce positive actions. Encourage students to pick up others' papers when they fall to the floor. Ask students to hand out materials to each other. Be direct: if you know of a student who gets picked on, ask another student to take him a pencil that you have provided. Simple gestures can make a world of difference in some students' lives.

- Although it is difficult, address students' power plays, mean comments, and inappropriate gestures and facial expressions. When they occur, confront students and discuss it with them right away.

- Empower students with tasks that make them leaders of groups, events, or daily tasks. Make them responsible for duties or organizational tasks.

- Create building-wide programs that focus on all members of the school community supporting each other. Various-colored wristbands have become popular; why not have your school use them to show support for each other?

- Create an advisory program or curriculum focused on helping others.

Questions for Reflections

1. Keep notes about your perception of your energy level and that of your students. How are they related? What inference can you make from this?

2. Keep a record of how much class time is used taking roll, passing papers in and out, and other "housekeeping" tasks. How does this impact students' motivation?

3. List any barriers to your implementing the Student Empowerment activity (Figure 6-1) in your class and brainstorm solutions with a colleague.

4. Keep track of students' power plays and the number of times you can and do intervene. What are barriers to intervening? With a colleague, brainstorm how to overcome those barriers.

5. How would you rate your school community in terms of supportiveness toward each other? Is helping others a norm? Is it modeled and practiced frequently by the faculty?

chapter VII

Discipline Proactively

Mr. Berckemeyer, why do you always say that you are always right?

Many times, without even knowing it, classroom teachers let our power slip away. In many cases, we lose the self-confidence to deal with inappropriate comments. Perhaps we feel a lack of support from others or worry what parents will think. So we allow students to treat us with disrespect. This has to stop. We need to talk as colleagues and teammates about how we deal with these inappropriate behaviors. Working together as a faculty, we can build respect based on the needs of our students and the safety of our teachers. We are responsible for more than curriculum; we are enforcers, nurses, caretakers, adoptive parents, and counselors. It's not an easy job. But working together, we can solve some of the power issues.

Managing classroom disruptions

Ultimately, the goal of classroom discipline is to help students learn to manage their own behavior, so your interventions must allow the student to correct the misbehavior with as little fuss as possible. The more overt and teacher-centered the intervention, the more sensitivity to peers, defensiveness, and lost learning time result. Following several guidelines for in-class interventions for disruptive behavior can increase your effectiveness and your classes' ability to focus on their goals. When a student disrupts class, and you must intervene,

- Keep it brief. Talking too much can lead to a power struggle; say as little as possible before refocusing students.

- Keep it private. Preserve their standing in their peers' eyes.

- Keep it impersonal. By focusing on the behavior and not the student, you increase chances for compliance and reduce chances of students becoming defensive. Also, don't bring up past misbehaviors; concentrating on the present encourages a quick resolution and can help avoid the situation escalating into a larger problem.

- Allow feelings. Make sure students know that you know they have a right to their feelings—whatever they may be. Help them learn to mange their behaviors to meet your classroom expectations regardless of their anger or frustration. This is an extremely important life and career skill that could benefit them as much as the content you teach them.

- First try ignoring the behavior (unless it is a safety or bullying issue), moving closer to the student or using facial cues to communicate your message.

- Give students a choice to stop disrupting or suffer the logical consequences of their behavior. The consequences should be proportional to the offensive behavior and specific. Firmly follow through with the consequence and then make a clean sweep of it. The student has then paid the dues and is on firm ground again.

Proactive versus reactive discipline

Proactively manage your classroom by removing potential causes of student misbehavior: have all the necessary materials ready and accessible at the start of class; plan and test all your activities and lessons. Imagine where your students may take the lesson and think through how far students can "run" with it before the outcome will not deliver the needed educational benefits. Set clear expectations for behavior and learning and vary the pace of the lesson to keep students engaged.

Michael Yell, a National Board Certified teacher at Hudson Middle School in Wisconsin, gives this "best piece of advice you could offer a new teacher about classroom management":

> Four words sum up the best advice on classroom management in my opinion: *It's all about engagement!!!!*

> Although I do not at all recommend this to others, I have not said or done anything regarding rules in my 7th grade classes for years. Far more important, I believe, is that from day one you engage your students in their learning. Continually be adding to your repertoire of active and engaging teaching strategies. Get kids up and moving, interacting, and discussing every day. Use manipulatives and vary, vary, vary. Invest some time weekly in class-building activities and, more often than that, begin your class with a warm-up.

Mike goes on to urge teachers to work with and adapt the strategies in the following books to fully engage students.

> *Cooperative Learning* by Spencer Kagan, one of the original cooperative learning gurus, features 200 cooperative learning strategies that can make even the most traditional lesson come alive for kids. I also strongly recommend his books *Classbuilding, Teambuilding*, and his books that are content area specific. His *Silly Sports and Goofy Games* is GREAT for warm-ups and advisory activities!
> *Everyone's Invited: Interactive Strategies that Engage Young Adolescents* by Jill Spencer, a middle school veteran of 30 years, has dozens of ideas and strategies for engaging your middle school students.
>
> *Summarization in Any Subject: 50 Techniques to Improve Student Learning* by Rick Wormeli includes 50 strategies you can easily add to your repertoire.
>
> from Middle Talk posting July 14, 2009

In contrast, an example of reactive discipline is writing a student up for coming to class without the necessary materials. Writing up students for misbehaving, not having materials, or being disrespectful is a reactive discipline method. By the time you write the referral, you have truly had enough. Your blood pressure is off the scale, your left eyelid is twitching, and your right hand is starting to shake. You might even be considered irrational at that point. But, if you react by first sending students to the office, you have few options left for later interventions that may be necessary.

Examples

Example 1: Let's say you have a student who is acting a little moodier or slightly more disrespectful than usual or is completely off task. Options for proactive discipline are talking with the student, making a phone call home, keeping him after class to finish work, and inviting him to your team meeting to discuss the situation. Or, you can ignore it and not worry that he might fail this semester; you might even decide to write up the student and let the office handle the student.

Example 2: You hand out an assignment to a student who says, "Ms. Fante, this is stupid. I hate this class." Because this is an atypical response from this particular student, you reprimand the student by saying, "Marina, this is not appropriate behavior." The student shrugs off the comment while continuing to give you the evil look embedded in every adolescent's eyeballs. The following day Marina again says she hates the class and that the assignment is so stupid a monkey could do it. As your anger rises, you think, "If it is so easy that a monkey could do it, then you should have no problem with it." Your feelings may be hurt, you may feel threatened by her hostility to your lesson idea— after all, this is a good kid. Two weeks ago she was making great contributions to the class, paying attention, and completing her work. What has changed? When the pattern is repeated again the next day, you lose your composure and send Marina to the office with a write-up for being disrespectful, not completing her work, and being off task.

Before you send Marina with the referral to the office, ask her to stay after class. With the referral in front of the student, discuss it with her, mentioning you are wondering about her sudden change in attitude and why she is being so disrespectful toward you. Give her options of talking with you about the issues or going to the office. Typically, adolescents respond, "I don't care." You might respond, "Look, I am trying to help you out. Why don't you sit down and think about what you want to do with this discipline write-up." After the student has had time to reflect, ask for her decision. "Do you want to talk about the discipline form or go to the office?" If she responds again by saying, "I don't care," take her to the office and have her sit there for a few minutes. Inform your principal or assistant principal about the student's change in attitude and tell him or her you want to chat with the student later in the day.

"Great middle grades educators know that if you do not handle the social and emotional needs of a young adolescent, you will never get to her academic needs."

Usually, offered the choice to talk about the issue, she will eventually break down, and the drama will begin: "Ms. Fante, I have been having such a bad week; my friends have been making fun of me and saying I did something I did not do. They are spreading horrible rumors about me." So you talk to the student, emphasizing stopping the inappropriate conduct in class and reassuring her that you will work together to solve the personal issue. Great middle level educators know that if you do not handle the social and emotional needs of a young adolescent, you will never get to her academic needs.

Talking to a student prior to making a referral is critical for your success as a middle level teacher. Yes, it takes time to do the follow-up; yes, it takes time, patience, and effort to talk with the student about what is happening in his or her life. However, the bottom line is that just sending him or her to the office does nothing for you and nothing for the student—it does not improve your relationship with the student, nor does it increase the student's trust in you and other adults. It just gives someone else the opportunity to solve the real problem.

The most important rule of teaching young adolescents is that no one magic solution solves everything, especially regarding discipline. Try several different approaches, modify when necessary, and more important, always do some form of follow through. Because your team also plays a critical role in classroom management, work with your team to help set academic and behavioral expectations. Working as a team to create solutions to discipline problems makes a huge difference.

Teacher responses to power plays

When conflict arises within the classroom, teachers tend to want to throw the responsible student(s) out of the classroom: Let the office deal with her! However, when we send a student to the office, we lose some of our power. How many times have we said to a student, "I am sending you to the office. And when you get back, I will also be talking to you about a consequence"? Time and time again, teachers say, "I sent her to the office, and THEY did nothing." First observation: administrators will never be as mad as you are. No matter how many times you underline or how many words you bold on the discipline form, an administrator will not be as emotional as you are. First piece of advice: Never write the referral in the heat of passion. Teachers have been known to write a referral with 23 exclamation marks on the form. Second piece of advice: Watch what you say on the referral form. Once, I wrote on a referral, "I am so sick, I am sick." My principal, who had a great sense of humor, wrote back on the form, "You are also redundant." Compared to some referrals sent to the office, this one was mild—just ask any administrator to see his or her file of classic referrals submitted by irrational teachers.

Things to ponder:

When referring a student to the office for using inappropriate language, just leave it at "inappropriate language; call me for details." During a phone call with a parent, you can then mention the word if they ask for it, or you can tell your administrator.

Take time to follow up with your students after you have written a referral. Explaining how their actions might be offensive or disrespectful, you can use it as a teachable moment. Remember: If you throw a kid out 30 times, he comes back 31 times, unless he moves.

When you are preparing to talk with parents, do not plan on them having an "aha moment." Parents tend to know if their child is unorganized, because they see their room every day. Parents see their child's disrespectful attitude toward others, and parents even know their child is late, lazy, or unprepared. Although they might not want to admit to these issues, chances are parents do know they exist.

Escalating misbehaviors

Admitting fault in front of their peers is very difficult for young adolescents—it's the last thing they want to do. Rather than taking ownership or responsibility for their actions, they find it easier to blame other students or the teacher. A typical classroom situation: Realizing he has forgotten the homework assignment, a student comes out with, "Mr. Toombs, this class is stupid, and you wore the same pants three days in a row." Isn't it interesting how young adolescents can remember your weekly clothing options, but they cannot remember the homework assignment from yesterday? Their fear of admitting a fault in front of their peers causes them to attack other students or the teacher.

No matter the situation or your level of frustration, never embarrass or belittle a student by ridiculing her or using sarcasm. Maintain your poise and refocus the student. Cornering a student with sarcasm or other aggressive behavior can cause middle school students to attack. Fear drives young adolescents to go for the jugular; they know and successfully exploit our biggest flaws. Constantly worried about what they should or might say or do and how they are and will be perceived by others in the room, they find that the easiest target of all is the teacher. When they attack the teacher, other students take notice and find it humorous, thus providing the student with needed attention.

Let's take a simple classroom situation and watch how it can escalate throughout the day. Say for example, Kristan comes to her first-hour class with no homework for the fifth time in a row. Having had enough, you point out the obvious reason for her lack of success in your class. As you are doing this, her classmates are hearing your judgment as, "Kristan, I am tired of this lazy behavior" or "I am sick of reminding you constantly about doing your work." Essentially, you have taken the student's power away and embarrassed her; you have increased her fear of nonacceptance by her peers. More important, she fears the other students now see her as weaker and that they will make a point to deprive her of even more power.

During second period, with its cooperative learning activities, Kristan tries to join a group of other students who let her know that they don't want her in the group because her laziness won't help them get a good grade. Again, people are taking her power away. In third hour, Kristan finds a weaker student or the easy target of the class, and she sees a way to get her power back; so she pounces on that student like a tiger on fresh kill. If a teacher observes her harassing another student, Kristan will hear, "Stop that! You need to stop picking on other students." We are once again back to the power play.

Later in the hallway on the way to another class, Kristan pushes another student while her first-hour teacher observes and responds, "Kristan, that is enough. You have not been doing your work, and now you are bullying other kids." Off to the office she goes. The teacher took away Kristan's power, and her goal was to get it back by any means. This problematic scenario happens all the time in our schools: a student is not working, a teacher uses too much power/takes away all the student's power, and a weaker student ends up getting pushed and bullied.

Because we teachers have very little or no time to reflect on such situations that are repeated throughout our days, we react and move on; we are busy, and we are trying to do the best we can. However, our students spend many waking hours in fear—fear of their peers, parents, and teachers. Here are some ideas for handling escalating situations:

- Teacher one-on-ones. If we educators confront a student in front of others, we might feel better or think we are setting an example for others, but what does that do to the student? Take time to talk to your students before or after class. Or even take a minute to talk to them at your desk. The conversations should be between you and the student, not you, the student, and the class.

- Follow up with other teachers and explain what kind of day the student is having. This can help teachers look out for that student and her interactions with other students.

- Look for ways to empower students in your classroom by having them help with tasks you need performed. Helping instills power in kids. Give a task or responsibility to the ones who tend to bully and who need to demonstrate their power to their peers.

- Address issues of bullying and the desire to pick on the less powerful right away. Bring the child into your team meeting to talk about the issues and keep the school counselor and principal in the loop.

- Encourage the school counselor to establish some mentoring programs for your students.

- Back off for a few moments. Offer the hall pass to the student, suggest getting a drink of water, or encourage the student to go to the restroom and splash some water on his or her face. Encourage the student to come back when he or she is ready, reminding the student you are watching the clock.

And, finally, just skip the silly rules. In the words of Robyn Jackson's "Setting Classroom Rules" (retrieved July 14, 2009, at www.mindstepsinc.com)

Honestly, most classroom rules I have seen range from unnecessary to downright silly. Do you really need to make it a rule that students bring their books to class? If they don't, is lunch detention really going to solve the problem? Wouldn't it be easier to just give them a book and move on?

Questions for Reflection

1. Think about a discipline problem you have recently handled; was your handling more reactive or proactive? How could you have improved your response?

2. Write the above problem and write the proactive solution you think would be the most effective, appropriate response. Plan to practice a similar response when the next discipline issue arises.

3. Recall an experience of a student's escalating misbehaviors. What might the result have been had a more proactive, student-centered intervention taken place.?

4. For 3 days keep a record of the times you think follow-ups with students regarding behavior problems were necessary but left undone. With a colleague, discuss possible solutions to the barriers.

5. For 3 days keep a record of the interventions you make for behavior problems. Then, highlight the behavior problems that, given the big picture, do not make a serious negative impact on students' learning. Reflect on how not making an issue of these problems would affect your teaching and students' learning.

chapter VIII

Suave Discipline

Mr. Berckemeyer, send me to the office—they are nicer to me there.

There are several schools of thought on classroom discipline. One view empowers teams or teachers to issue major consequences when necessary. If you think that is the administration's job, this may seem radical and confusing. However, when adolescents say, "They suspended me," they view the office personnel, dean of students, assistant principal, or principal, as the primary disciplinarian. The office, not the teacher. Teachers: we have given up some of our power and we need to reclaim it by ensuring that middle school students consider us the primary disciplinarians.

Although great middle schools, teachers, and administrators work together to solve problems that arise, the teacher or team should determine and follow through with consequences for inappropriate behavior. Not an easy task, this takes time and trust. Let's be honest, sometimes we teachers are not the most rational people when dealing with troublesome students, because we are the ones directly involved with their acting out. If teachers had all the power of meeting out consequences, they would sometimes overreact. A 10-week suspension might seem logical sometimes— even if there are only five weeks of school remaining! You think the student's future teaching team owes you, because the student's sentence will run through the first five weeks of school next year. Because no one is rational all the time, teams, teachers, and administrators must work together to solve problems.

When teachers take ownership of classroom management,

- The teacher decides and communicates consequences for behavior; the teacher facilitates the follow-through with the student.
- The teacher feels empowered.
- The teacher communicates with the student and family or caretakers involved.
- Students view the teacher as the primary disciplinarian.
- The teacher controls and handles student make-up work or missing assignments.
- The teacher can involve the student, parents, and administrators in figuring out how best to help the student.
- There is more discussion about student behavior.
- The teacher becomes the student advocate.
- Of course for offenses such as vandalism; fighting; swearing; and drug, smoking, and alcohol problems, the school administration typically handles the discipline.

A five-step plan

A five-step plan for teachers, schools, and administrators to share ownership of classroom management issues is

> Step 1: Document
>
> Step 2: Meet as a team with student
>
> Step 3: Create a list of strategies
>
> Step 4: Inform parents and administrators
>
> Step 5: Provide follow-up

Step 1 Document

When receiving certification, every school administrator has a magic chip placed in his or her head. Thereafter, when a teacher says, "I am having problems with Olivia," the chip automatically engages, causing the administrator to say, "Did you call the parent?" Calling the parent is the first line of defense, and you should document the call regardless of the outcome.

Keep a record of general student information about each student in a place where any team member can easily access it. Having it handy enables the teacher to make the call before it becomes ancient history and the student has moved on to further incidents. Use the following figure to collect contact information for each student's parent or guardian.

Figure 8-1

Home Contact Information — Grade 6 Team   Year _____

General Student Information

Student Name _____   HR _____

Parent Names _____

_____

Other contact names and relationship to student _____

_____

Phone numbers for contacts:

#1 _____ #2 _____ #3_____

E-mail: E1 _____ E2 _____

The team needs to be aware of:

Have you ever had a call to a parent about misbehavior backfire? "Ms. Clark, this is Mr. Berckemeyer calling from Scott Carpenter Middle School about your daughter Olivia. Yesterday she used some inappropriate language with me and become a little violent." The parent responds, "Oh, Mr. Berckemeyer, I am glad you called. Olivia comes home every night crying because you are picking on her." Suddenly, you are the one in trouble—and then you backpedal, saying, "I will talk to her about these issues." The parent replies, "Good, because if you don't, I will call the principal. Besides, she gets along with all her other teachers!"

Forms for documenting all calls and meetings with parents and guardians help build a case history about a student's behavioral and academic growth. The history of calls, meetings, and conversations helps the team and the parents collaborate on solutions to meet a student's needs and is an easy way to keep administrators advised about the strategies employed and seek their input.

Modify the communications form in Figure 8-2 to meet your team and school needs. You can keep the log in a notebook or, even better, create a file for every student and put the communication log in each file.

Step 2 Team meets with students
Teachers' lounge discussions and team meetings can become unproductive venting sessions, accomplishing nothing. How many times have you walked out of a team meeting and said, "That was the biggest waste of time!" Either the team focused too much time on one student, or there was no resolution to the problem.

Figure 8-2

Communication Log — 6th Grade Team   Year _____

Date: _____   Teacher _____

Letter sent ☐

Meeting held ☐

Phone conference ☐ Number called: _____ Spoke to: _____

E-mail ☐   Address used _____ E-mail Recipient _____

Reason:

Results/action taken:

Who is responsible for action?

Date for outcome of action:

When dealing with student issues, teachers and teams can adopt several rules to become effective. **Rule one: The team gets three free vents about every student.** After a student's behaviors have been vented three times, the team must come up with three ideas to solve the problems. If you don't take this action, you will be talking about this same student and this student's same behaviors until the end of the school year. Of course, you must implement the strategies you came up with. If the ideas fail, or you go back to venting about that child, you must come up with three more ideas. This technique just might stop the complaining and may result in a solution for the problem.

Bring students into the team meeting

Empowered middle level educators involve students in every aspect of their daily school lives including classroom management. Often some students go from class to class causing misery and chaos wherever they alight: a nervous breakdown for the first period teacher, a popped blood vessel in the eyeball for the second period teacher, and a relapse to smoking and a nervous tick for the third period teacher! Needless to say, the student's fourth period teacher will retire early, and she has only taught for four years! This is a normal day for some young adolescents. If you happen to walk into the teachers' lounge and merely mention that student's name, one teacher passes out, one gets up to go smoke, and two others just sit there with dazed, confused looks on their faces. Meanwhile, the student is enjoying lunch, looking forward to the electives coming up in the afternoon.

Bring the student to the team meeting. When it's time for the meeting to start, go to his elective classroom and ask if you can borrow him for a few minutes. Nine times out of ten, the elective teacher will tell you to keep him for the entire hour. Sending a note saying the core team requires the presence of this student appears rude and disrespects the elective teachers. Walking down to the room opens up communication and allows you to walk back with the student. You would be amazed at how much you can accomplish by walking from the band room to the 7th grade hall with the student who will be attending the team meeting. After the team meeting, have the student fill out a Student Reflection Sheet, such as that shown in Figure 8-3, before he or she returns for a follow-up team meeting. Especially important is the question asking how the student's behavior helped or hurt the situation.

Step 3 Create a list of strategies

Before the student attends the meeting, you and your teammates should identify three things on which you want the student to work. Resist the urge to create a list of 50 things you want changed by tomorrow. Remember: the student is an adolescent who, by definition, has only been alive for 10 to 15 years. Mistakes will be made; authority will be challenged; "what the big deal is" will be a mystery. So focus on only three things. The most critical piece of this is: when choosing the three items, do not mix academic issues with behavior issues. Focus on one or the other. Young adolescents have difficulty making the connection between the two.

Figure 8-3

Student Behavior Reflection Sheet   Year _____

Name _____ Class/Period _____ Date_____

Describe the situation that happened:

How did your behavior help or hurt the situation?

If you had a chance to do it all over again, what would you have done

differently?

What consequences should be given?

What ideas do you have to make sure this situation does not happen again?

Teacher/Team Notes

Consequences given:

Additional comments:

Team Member _____ Student _____

Also critical is the adolescent's engaging in the conversation about his or her behavior or academic performance; the student collaborates on decision making, and, ultimately, the student will be held accountable for following through. Academic issues can include

Not completing work

Too much time off task

Late assignments

Incomplete work

Not doing their own work

Lack of participation during class

Missing vast amounts of class work due to absences

Missing homework

An example of a form for logging all academic interventions made for a student is shown in Figure 8-4. Revise it as necessary to reflect your intervention strategies.

A sample log form for interventions for behavioral issues is shown in Figure 8-5. Behavioral issues can include bothering others, bullying, disrespecting the teacher or other students, coming to class without materials, roaming, disrupting class, and using inappropriate humor. A sample log form for interventions for behavioral issues is shown in Figure 8-5.

Holding students accountable is the difficult part. The teacher must remind students of their commitments to improve. If a student misses an obligation, as soon as the student arrives the next day, remind the student of the expectations created

Figure 8-4

Academic Intervention Log

Student Name _____ Homeroom_____

Academic challenges observed by team or teacher: _____
_____
_____
_____

Classroom Teacher Intervention	Date/Team Member
• Conference with student	_____
• Sign agenda book before the student leaves class	_____
• Phone call with parent	_____
• Parent meeting at school with student and teachers	_____
• Daily progress report given and sent home with student	_____
• Use of a peer tutor	_____
• Modified assignment	_____
• Notes provided for the student	_____
• Have student repeat directions to the teacher	_____
• Weekly teacher assistance	_____
• Cleaning out notebook	
• Cleaning out locker or desk	
• Cleaning out backpack	
• Provide help at lunch or after school	_____
• Verbal checks for understanding	_____
• Use of advanced organizers	_____
• Plan of improvement created and follow-up assigned	_____
• Provide an adult mentor	_____
• Team study hall recommended	_____
• Pace instruction differently for the student	_____
• Offer alternative assessment or assignment	_____

Figure 8-4 (continued)

Academic Intervention Log — (continued)

Classroom Teacher Intervention	Date/Team Member
• Hold a child study meeting with counselors and other support staff	_____
• Team discussion about student	_____
• Have student attend team meeting – establish goals with students and timeline	_____

Student Responsibilities

• Fill out missing assignment sheet when work is not completed	_____
• Record homework and assignments in student agenda or planner	_____
• Attend help sessions at lunch or before or after school	_____
• Organize binder and notebook	_____
• Clean out locker or desk	_____
• Clean out backpack on a weekly basis	_____
• Seek help and support when needed	_____
• Start work and see what can be accomplished before asking for help	_____
• Ask another student for help or advice	_____

Parent Involvement

• Provide tutoring	_____
• Check student planner or agenda nightly	_____
• Clean out backpack and notebooks	_____
• Meet with team	_____
• Conference call with team on a weekly basis	_____
• Set up study time at home	_____
• Call teachers when concerns arise	_____
• Set up monthly meeting with school counselor and support team	_____

Figure 8-5

Behavior Interventions

Student Name _____ Homeroom_____

Behavior issues observed by team or teacher: _____
_____
_____
_____

Teacher Interventions	Date/Team Member
• Preferred seating	_____
• Close to teacher	
• Center of the room or front	
• Positive reinforcement for desired behaviors	_____
• Lunch detention	_____
• After school detention	_____
• Conference with student	_____
• Phone call to parent	_____
• Team meeting with student	_____
• Assign an adult mentor or student mentor	_____
• Referral	_____
• One-on-one meeting with student and a teacher	_____
• Meeting with support staff and counselor	_____
• Hold a child study meeting	_____
• Create a behavior contract	_____
• Suggest in-school suspension	_____
• Saturday school	_____
• Suggest out-of-school suspension	_____
• Establish rewards	_____

---

during the team meeting. Remind the student of the goal of four good days or two good weeks of following the agreed-upon plan. (Keep the time goal short: none of this "Behave for the rest of your life" stuff.) Because adolescents need reminders, each teacher on the team should follow this procedure for several

Figure 8-5 (continued)

Behavior Interventions — (continued)

Teacher Interventions	Date/Team Member
Student Responsibility	
• Communicate with teacher when angry or frustrated before acting out	_____
• Use a time out area	_____
• Use conflict resolution	_____
• Use a self-reminder system when acting out	_____
• Isolate yourself when angry	_____
• Talk to an adult when needing advice on how to handle peers or other issues	_____
• Self-monitor behavior contract	
• Seek out positive reinforcement from peers and teachers	_____ _____
Parent Responsibility	
• Communicate with teachers	_____
• Attend team meetings	_____
• Come to school with child	_____
• Discuss issues with counselor or support staff	_____ _____
• Follow up with behavior contract	
• Offer rewards	_____
• Stay consistent	_____ _____

days. You might even need to bring the student back in for a "team talk." Reminders are key; yes, they take time, but we must hold adolescents accountable. When the student has lived up to the agreement, thank him or her for the great effort. One teacher says of having students attending team meetings:

This has really worked on our team. We let the teen know we would do whatever was necessary to help him or her with behavior or academics; they knew we meant it. They would work out a strategy for improvement with us that was reasonable. If it didn't work, we called her or him back in to meet with us again. Only one student had to come back for regrouping.

Teacher Jean Huffman in an e-mail May 31, 2009

Make sure you also establish a reward system for the student. Set up the expectation and time frame, and then provide the student with the reward date. Adolescents respond to many types of rewards for good behavior.

- A reward that the student selects. Students might ask for things you cannot provide or that are not fair, but knowing what motivates that child is good information.

- Time. Young adolescents love extra time for work, extra time between classes, time to talk to with friends, or 5 minutes playing basketball with a friend or a teacher.

- Simple rewards such as snacks. Healthful snacks may not be the most popular, but many adolescents will eat almost anything.

- Attention from the teacher. Some students may want to spend time with a particular teacher at lunch, which can then become a punishment for the teacher. However, spending the time with a student can make a world of difference to him or her.

The best rewards involve time and interaction. In spite of the popularity of food and drinks as rewards, the bottom line is that most kids cause problems to get attention. Think of rewards that offer the most precious gift—your time.

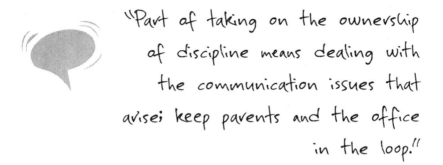

"Part of taking on the ownership of discipline means dealing with the communication issues that arise; keep parents and the office in the loop."

Some students may need more than 10 team meetings; others, one or two meetings. You know your kids, and you know what works. If the student lives up to the expectations for the agreed upon amount of time, invite the student to a team meeting to talk about his or her accomplishment and the reward that he or she has earned. And for the class as a whole, reviewing class rules periodically through puzzles or Jeopardy keeps them fresh in students' minds.

Empower students in team meetings

Team meetings are not just for students who have misbehaved. You can also use the team talk to motivate and involve your students. "Team talk" is an important strategy that works by empowering students and giving them a voice in school life. Here are some other ways to involve students in your team meetings.

- Following a lesson, unit, or project, invite students to a team meeting to discuss the project or event. Empower your students by asking for their input on the subject matter, the assignments, or the final project—much like a focus group. If they know you are open to their honest feedback, most adolescents will share their opinions and discuss their likes and dislikes concerning the lesson.

- At the year's end, meet with a group of students who have performed well all year. Having them share what they liked about the year will be a great boost for you and your students. It might even stop your eyelid twitch or your lip quiver for a few days.

- Involve students in helping create a unit of study; they can participate in team meetings, devising lessons and activities.

- Have students practice their social and presentation skills by bringing their ideas for rewards and celebrations to the team.

- Students can practice problem solving and collaboration by sharing ideas about how to spruce up the hallways, eliminate tardiness, or clean up perpetual messes in the lunchroom or hallways.

Finally, remember to document the time a student spends in your team meeting; at many schools this is done online for easy access by all team members and the guidance counselor. You and your team will need this information as you collaborate throughout the year with the students' parents or guardians and the administration on academic and behavior improvements. Some schools have parents or guardians join the team's meeting with the student.

Step 4: Inform parents and administrators plus Step 5: Follow-up

After the student attends the team meeting, talk with your administrator and call the parents with the results of the meeting; then schedule a meeting of the team, student, and parents to discuss the issues and the student's improvement plan. It never hurts to over-communicate, and again, make sure your documentation is current.

The final, and essential, step is to follow up. Even if the student and parent leave the meeting with responsibilities, as the teacher, you will be responsible for holding people accountable. Let the student know you are supporting efforts at improvement. Use positive reinforcement, remind the student if he or she makes a misstep, and fully recognize reaching goals and meeting commitments. Learning to manage behavior is key to later success in a career and life in general.

In providing such support, you are making a critical difference in the young adolescent's life as explained in *This We Believe: Keys to Educating Young Adolescents* (2009).

> The "hidden curriculum"—what students learn indirectly but surely from the people with whom they interact, the structures in which they work, and the issues that inevitably occur in a human

enterprise—has a powerful influence on students' education. In fact, this aspect of learning is sometimes so profound and long lasting that it overrides learning that is more traditional. Lives are often shaped more by small individual actions, probing questions, subtle reminders, earned commendations, and personalized challenges, than by direct instruction. (p. 29)

Working Lunch: Alternative to detention

A viable alternative to after-school detention is the Working Lunch program, which has been used with success by holding students accountable for improving their behavior while depriving them of cherished free time with peers. Behaviors such as not working in class, not submitting homework, and minor class disruptions are recorded on a Working Lunch Admittance Form, which states the infraction and the assignment that the student is to complete during lunchtime. The teacher assigning the Working Lunch is responsible for phoning the student's parents or guardian. Students sign the form and receive their pass to Working Lunch, which states the guidelines: students report directly to the working lunch classroom and are not allowed in the cafeteria; they may bring a bag lunch or purchase a lunch that will be provided by the cafeteria; tardiness or disruptions result in an additional day of working lunch. The teaching team handles a student's first six problems using working lunches, team conference meetings, guidance referral, and e-mailing and calling parents. After the sixth intervention, teachers refer the student to the office with a recommendation for suspension. The guidance counselor is notified, and the parent or guardian is invited to meet with the teachers.

Figure 8-6

Working Lunch Admittance Form

Name _____ Lunch Period _____ ID# _____

Grade _____ Team _____ Period Infraction Occured _____

Parent or Guardian to contact _____ Phone#_____
                                                (work or home)

Teacher assigning working lunch _____

Date of working lunch _____

Reason:

Assignments to be completed:

Teacher signature _____ Date: _____

*** Please attach all work to be completed at Working Lunch to this form. ***

Figure 8-7

Working Lunch Pass

_____has been assigned a working lunch on _____

And will report to room 133 during lunch period.

I understand that Working Lunch has been assigned as indicated above and

that I am to complete assignments provided by the teacher.

Student signature _____ Date _____

- -

Working Lunch Guidelines:

1. Students are to report directly to Room 133 during their lunch period.
   (You are not allowed in the cafeteria for any reason.)

2. Students may bring a bag lunch or purchase a lunch provided by the
   cafeteria.

3. Students are to sit in the seat assigned by the Working Lunch directors.

4. Any tardiness, talking, or disruptive behavior will result in an "instant
   replay," which will result in an additional day of Working Lunch.

5. Students receiving their seventh Working Lunch will be referred to the
   office and recommended for suspension.

Teachers at Madison Junior High School in Mansfield, OH, who modified the idea given to them by Mike Occhipinti to fit their school's goals, take turns supervising Working Lunch, and report that the losing of the privilege of spending lunchtime with friends is a tremendous motivator in changing behavior. See Figure 8-6 for the basic Working Lunch form and Figure 8-7 for the student pass into Working Lunch.

Student accountability

In *Meet Me in the Middle* (2001), Rick Wormeli discusses accountability as a benchmark of behavior and giving students standards to guide their decision making. He suggests students use these five questions to test out the viability of an ethical decision:

1. Am I making this choice with the hope that no one will find out?

2. How will I look back on this choice ten years from now?

3. Am I doing to others what I would want them to do to me?

4. If [an admired person] were in the same situation, what would he or she do?

5. If everyone were about to do what I'm going to do, would I want to live in the world shaped by that decision? (p. 61)

Questions for Reflection

1. Are teachers and teams in your school empowered to handle discipline problems? If not, what are barriers to this and how can they be overcome? If so, what issues still need to be resolved?

2. Are your documentation procedures effective and used consistently? If not, what needs to happen to improve this part of the discipline process?

3. Do your current discipline processes empower students to be accountable for their actions? What improvements would encourage students to take responsibility?

4. Why is it critical for the teacher to be viewed as the primary disciplinarian?

5. For one week keep a record of the percentage of school meeting time that is spent discussing students' misbehavior. Is this a reasonable percentage? If not, identify opportunities for improving it.

chapter IX

Manage Classroom Interruptions

Mr. Berckemeyer, can we have a free day?

Although some strategies for addressing classroom interruptions passed down from teaching generation to teaching generation might still work today, many have been figured out by this generation of students and are no longer effective.

Have you ever ... ?

Have you ever said, "I will never do that in my classroom," but then find yourself doing that very thing?

- Saying "Shhh." If you make the noise long enough, you will run out of air and then pass out. And you know as your lifeless body hits the ground, the kids are thinking: "Free day!" Instead, have the students take a deep breath and then let it out. Have them do this several times in hopes that they will relax and quiet themselves.

- Ignoring the behavior. Many times, we choose just to ignore inappropriate behavior in hopes that the student will stop. Instead, offer a consequence—"If you don't stop, I am going to ...." Don't be afraid to be over the top with your consequences; just make sure they are appropriate. But here is the rule: If you say it, you have to follow through. Let's say, for example, that you offer a consequence, the student repeats the act, but you do not act on it. You have now sent a clear message to that student and the rest of the class: you do not follow through with consequences; this sets you up for many discipline struggles to come.

- Flicking the lights. Although this strategy might still work in some cases, if you do it more than 10 times, the students think it is a disco ball, and they start to dance.

Do try these...

Try these unique ideas in your classroom and spend time reflecting on some of your not-so-effective strategies. Some of these strategies take high self-esteem on your part and a personality comfortable with using humor. When you try them, your students might run out of class thinking you need some professional help. Then again, maybe that is not a bad thing.

- Have a conversation with the chalkboard: The next time your students are not listening, walk over to the chalkboard and say, "Oh chalkboard, you will listen to me. You're the reason I became a teacher. I love you chalkboard..." Students will say to each other, "Is he

talking to the chalkboard?" "Shh! It must be important."
When a teacher talks to an inanimate object, students
listen.

- Stand on a chair and recite poetry.

- Start talking with words that don't make sense. When
  students are not paying attention, just start talking
  gibberish. Talk as though you are from a foreign country,
  or even better, another planet.

- Use dry erase boards to have students provide answers.
  Place the dry erase boards under the chairs; next time
  you want your students to share an answer, have them
  write it down on the dry erase board. If they do not
  know the answer, have them put a question mark on
  the board. That way you will know if the kids are
  paying attention, and it is a great way to check for
  comprehension.

- Reprimand a student not in the room when a group is
  off task. It's difficult to identify just one student causing
  the distraction in a group, so you end up singling out
  the last student you observe talking about something
  other than the work. It goes down like this: "Bernice,
  enough is enough. You need to get back on task." Bernice
  defends herself (and rightly so): "Mr. Berckemeyer,
  everyone else in the group was talking just as much as I
  was, and you yelled at me and not the other kids!" Next
  time—just yell at a kid that is not in the room. "Bob,
  don't pretend I can't see you. Bob, I am so on the edge
  right now." Meanwhile, your students will be thinking,

"Who's Bob, and why is he in trouble?" There is nothing wrong with being emotionally unstable around young adolescents. Go ahead and act like you could snap at any time.

- Before automatically saying "no," listen to students. Even if the answer is still a big fat "no," we owe it to them to at least hear them out. Many times you can say, "I will let you go to the bathroom after we start the lesson and after you have finished a couple of the problems." This is a win/win situation—the student might come back up later to ask to go to the bathroom, but in most cases, he will forget, and you make sure he is completing his work.

- Communicate your limits. If you use humor often in your classroom, students may have trouble discerning whether you are joking or serious. So, establish a signal to communicate your limits. Use an expression or a phrase such as, "I am serious as a heart attack, you need to simmer down." Others give a physical signal such as kicking the wastebasket to mean, "I'm dead serious now." Giving them a cue will give them time to refocus and helps draw the line between class fun time and class focus time.

- Be consistent. No matter what your style or type of classroom management, the most important thing is to be consistent (unless your classroom is totally out of control; then, forget consistency and change things up a bit.) Consistency equals security. They want to feel confident that you can be counted on; when you are moody, it shakes their confidence in you! Adolescents crave consistency. In many cases, teachers are the most stable thing in an adolescent's life.

- Be entertaining! Classrooms should be fun!

- Understand your students' lives. Many of your students come from unique backgrounds and experiences. They might have two very supportive parents—a mother who cares and is involved, and a father who helps out with the soccer team—or they may have two very committed mothers or fathers. Accept the diversity of backgrounds, home lives, and parent involvement that come with your students. Many of our students deal with divorce issues, parents who are ill, or no parents at all. Make sure you understand your students' lives. It can explain why they never do homework or why they never bring materials to class.

 "If you want kids to work, you have to work the room."

Specifically teach your students to be organized by using a system that you reinforce, monitor, and about which you provide feedback. Example: Each core team agrees on a trapper keeper for classes to keep their work in. Students can organize their pre-punched papers for each class in that class' particular color folder (for example, reading = blue). No book bags are allowed in classrooms—only the folders and writing tools. All the core classes are on the team floor and students' lockers are close to their classrooms. The three minutes between classes allow for no side activities when transitioning between classes. Assignment books must go to all classes to be completed and are the only way a student can leave a classroom because the hall pass slip is in the book. Each nine weeks, a student may use the hall pass 4 times in a core class. For continuity and consistency, each team member starts each class each day with the same routine—journaling, assignment book completion, and advance organizer.

Takeaways

Things well worth remembering are:

- Every great middle school teacher knows good teaching is all about relationships. The more you care about young adolescents, the easier it is to be an effective middle level educator. They make good company, they tell hilarious stories, they are kind and compassionate, and they are willing to help make a difference.

- Identify rude behavior. Don't overlook inappropriate comments. Don't pretend not to see a student trip another student in the hall. Don't walk away when you see a student breaking a school rule. Remember: It takes a village to raise a child; do your part.

- Talk to your students as a group about the expectations for good citizenship in your school as part of your responsibility to help foster ethical and caring individuals. When a student is rude or disrespectful, take the time to have a one-on-one talk.

- Use the power of wait time. Young adolescents need time to think, time to react, and more important, time to remember facts and information. Educators try to move at such a quick pace that sometimes they do not allow time for a young adolescent to think. The rule is a five-second wait time. Young adolescents might even need seven seconds. Be patient!

- Give affirmations. A subtle "Hello" or "Nice job" can make a difference in a young adolescent's life.

- Practice new materials in small amounts. When first introducing a topic, do not hand out a worksheet with 20 questions. Cut the worksheet in half. If they are overwhelmed from the start, students will just shut down; give them smaller portions of information they can digest.

- Enhance handouts with drawings or cartoons to help stimulate thinking. Make the content engaging without distracting them with clutter.

- Always be on the move. Yes, that means if you are the lover of the overhead projector, you need to give some attention to the other things in the room—the students. Constantly walking around the room allows you to monitor students' activities. The overhead projector does not need your attention—students need to feel your constant presence in the room.

- Don't put too much information on the overhead, interactive whiteboard, or PowerPoint. Monitor how much type you end up putting on visual teaching surfaces. Make it easy for students to figure out what problem you are working on or what word or phrase you are discussing. Clutter confuses your students, so keep the visual presentation simple.

- Adjust the type size on the overhead, interactive whiteboard, and PowerPoint so that students can easily read it from the back of the room—you may be surprised how small it looks from the back of the room. Use this rule for type size: place the transparency on the floor at your feet and then read it from a standing position. If you cannot read it, make the type size larger. If you need more space, use the blank wall above the whiteboard.

- Keep your hands clean. Fewer germs means fewer sick days, which results in fewer sub plans. Also, drink tons of water. According to ear, nose, and throat doctors, teaching is the number two profession for vocal chord abuse. (Singing is number one.)

- Never commit educational sabotage. Never say, "I don't care what you do in Ms. Yellico's class." Or, when students say, "Ms. Cervantes lets us," your normal reaction is, "Do I look like Ms. Cerrantes?" You may say something to imply other classes are not as important as yours. When you make statements disrespecting other teachers, you model that behavior for students. There are enough people bashing teachers; we need not do it to each other.

In closing

Starting our teaching careers with a wide-eyed sense of optimism, we all had a few ace-in-the-hole lessons sure to motivate young adolescents. We envisioned students sitting on the edges of their seats, drawn into our subject matter by their burning desire to know everything about gas, combustibles, and other things that blow up—and by our riveting teaching ability. This was our dream, the reason we went into teaching—to make a difference in the lives of each and every one of our students.

Then, reality sets in. We wonder why kids don't get excited about the hands-on lessons we have spent hours preparing. We get frustrated as our perfect lesson bombs. I created a lesson so cool I even wore an outrageous costume for dramatic effect, only to hear the familiar sounds of restless middle school students saying, "We did this last year. And Ms. Cervantes, our 6th grade teacher, wore a better costume."

I did not accept defeat. Nor did I take it personally. What I did do was teach the lesson five days later to the same students after making some adjustments. This time, they were a little more eager, and the lesson seemed to go over fairly well. You just never know how it is going to work out. So, keep on being creative and keep moving forward. Yes, there will be a daily barrage of adolescent angst. Yes, every lesson will be criticized before you even begin. Remember: as middle school students, in a little while their fear that everyone is watching them will slowly wither away, leaving you to engage them in creative activities. Never stop trying. Now, go out there and make a difference!

Questions for Reflection

1. What is your teaching style? How do young adolescents relate to you? What are your strengths and weaknesses in connecting with students?

2. Write two achievable goals for improving your classroom management effectiveness. Then write three specific actions you will take to accomplish each of them. Share this plan with a colleague and ask your colleague to check with you periodically to evaluate your progress and discuss the challenges you face.

References

Baenen, J., & Berckemeyer, J. (2005). *H.E.L.P. for teachers.* Westerville, OH: National Middle School Association.

Dyck, B. (2004). The *rebooting of a teacher's mind.* Westerville, OH: National Middle School Association.

Fodeman, D., & Monroe, M. (2009).*The impact of Facebook on our students.* Retrieved June 29, 2009, from http://www.nais.org/resources/article.cfm?ItemNumber=151505

Frey, N., & Fisher, D. (2008). The under-appreciated role of humiliation in the middle school. *Middle School Journal, 39*(3), 4-12.

Jackson, R. (2008). *Setting classroom rules.* Retrieved July 14, 2009, from http://www.mindstepsinc.com

Kagan, L., Kagan, M., & Kagan, S. (1995). *Classbuilding.* San Juan Capistrano, CA: Kagan Cooperative Learning.

Kagan, L., Kagan, M., & Kagan, S. (1997). *Teambuilding.* San Juan Capistrano, CA: Kagan Cooperative Learning.

Kagan, S. (1992). *Cooperative learning.* San Juan Capistrano, CA: Kagan Cooperative Learning.

Kagan, S., (1992). *Silly sports and goofy games.* San Juan Capistrano, CA: Kagan Cooperative Learning.

Nansel, T., Overpeck, M., Pilla, R., Ruan, W., Simons-Morton, B., & Scheidt, P. (2001). Bullying behaviors among U.S. youth: Prevalence and association with psychosocial adjustment. *Journal of the American Medical Association, 285*(16), 2094–2100.

National Middle School Association. (2010). *This we believe: Keys to educating young adolescents.* Westerville, OH: Author.

Ribble, M., & Bailey, G. (2007). *Digital citizenship in schools.* Eugene, OR, & Washington, DC: International Society for Technology in Education.

Spencer, J. (2008). *Everyone's invited! Interactive strategies that engage young adolescents.* Westerville, OH: National Middle School Association.

Van Hoose, J., Strahan, D., & L'Esperance, M. (2009). *Promoting harmony: Young adolescent development and classroom practices.* Westerville, OH: National Middle School Association.

Wormeli, R. (2003). *Day one & beyond.* Portland, ME, & Westerville, OH: Stenhouse & National Middle School Association.

Wormeli, R. (2007). *Differentiation: From planning to practice.* Portland, ME, & Westerville, OH: Stenhouse & National Middle School Association.

Wormeli, R. (2001). *Meet me in the middle.* Portland, ME, & Westerville, OH: Stenhouse & National Middle School Association.

Wormeli, R. (2004). *Summarization in any subject: 50 techniques to improve student learning.* Alexandria, VA: Association for Supervision and Curriculum Development.

About the Author

Jack C. Berckemeyer

Jack has taught language arts, social studies, health, expression skills, and physical education in Colorado middle schools. Named Outstanding Educator after two years of teaching at Scott Carpenter Middle School, Jack was identified as one of the outstanding educators in the Adams County School District, and in 2003 Falcon School District awarded him the Outstanding Alumni Award.

Known for his practical teaching strategies that engage and motivate young adolescents, Jack has thus far offered professional development presentations to middle level educators in 30 different national and international locations. Jack works with the 58 affiliate organizations of National Middle School Association throughout the world, and he co-authored *HELP for Teachers* and the NMSA Professional Development Kit, *The What, Why, and How of Student-Led Conferences*. Jack also coordinates on-site professional development for schools and school districts. For the last several years Jack has served as a judge for the Disney American Teacher Awards and as a selection committee member for the USA Today All Teacher Team.

A graduate of the University of Northern Colorado, Jack has a bachelor's degree in elementary and middle level education and a K–12 certification in school administration.

CPSIA information can be obtained at www.ICGtesting.com
Printed in the USA
BVOW012350030213

312194BV00005B/8/P